SCOTLAND THE BRAVE

JOHN LAFFIN

Scotland the Brave

The Story of the Scottish Soldier

WHITE LION PUBLISHERS
London, New York, Sydney and Toronto

Copyright © John Laffin, 1963

First published in the United Kingdom by
Cassell & Company Ltd., 1963

White Lion edition, 1974

ISBN 0 85617 106 9

Printed in Great Britain by
Biddles Ltd., Guildford, Surrey,
for White Lion Publishers Ltd.,
138 Park Lane, London W1Y 3DD

DEDICATED

TO THE MEMORY

OF ALL

HIGHLAND AND LOWLAND SOLDIERS

KILLED IN ACTION

WHILE SERVING IN THE

BRITISH ARMY

FOR MARIO

Preface

THIS IS not intended to be a history of Scots in arms, since several volumes would be necessary for such a task. It is, rather, an appreciation of the Scottish soldier, an attempt to show how his environment, his ancestry and his very nature combine to make him one of the finest fighting soldiers in history. While I have devoted a short chapter to the history of each of the Scottish regular regiments, my overall purpose—which is, quite frankly, to appraise and glorify the Jocks—has not been influenced by regimental considerations.

Inevitably, in a single book covering a period from the Middle Ages to the present day, I have had to be strictly selective in my material. Not every incident nor every personality could be included. Also, the emphasis is on the Scottish regular regiments while the service battalions, Territorials, Yeomanry and others are dealt with only in passing.

Some of the Highland regiments have, perhaps, the more colourful history, but it would be invidious to write only of Highland regiments, when some of the Lowland ones are distinctly older and when their service has been equally loyal. Once there were great differences of tradition between the two, but over the years these differences have become muted and some are now non-existent. To a large extent the history of one Scottish regiment is the history of all and each forms an integral part of the larger whole, of the Scottish military story. The twelve regiments complemented each other, as so often in their warlike history they fought beside each other. To non-Scotsmen they have all become 'the Jocks', and this nickname is now as valid for the Scottish soldier, Highland or Lowland, as the name 'Digger' is for Australian soldiers.

When I began work on this book a famous Scottish soldier, who is also a friend of mine, told me that no Scotsman could write such a book because his motives would be suspect and he would be open to a charge of bias. This hardly applies in my case, for I am an Australian and my opinions, I hope, will be accepted as sincere. Still, I confess to this—I would go into action any day in the ranks of a Scottish regiment and in all history I know of no finer soldier than the Jock.

Contents

[x]

Illustrations

The 93rd Highlanders assault the Shah Nujjif Mosque at Lucknow, 16 November 1857

Lieutenant Farquharson of the Black Watch winning the V.C. at Lucknow

Officers of the 21st (Royal North British Fusiliers) Regiment of Foot at Barbados, about 1862

The Dargai Heights

A machine-gun post of the 1st Cameronians outside a wood at Venizel, September 1914*

The Battle of Bazentin Ridge. An issue of rum to the Black Watch after the capture of Longueval, 14 July 1916*

Officers and men of the Gordon Highlanders resting by the roadside near Meaulte, July 1916*

Roll-call of Seaforth Highlanders on the afternoon of the first day of the Battle of the Somme—Beaumont-Hamel, 1 July 1916*

A patrol of the 1st Cameron Highlanders in action among the ruins of Cuinchy, 17 April 1918*

A Scots Guardsman giving a wounded prisoner a drink near Courcelles, August 1918*

A cairn commemorating members of the Black Watch killed in its vicinity on 21 November 1941—about six miles from Tobruk

A makeshift officers mess of the Highland Light Infantry just before going into action in the Desert, June 1942*

The 2nd Argyll and Sutherland Highlanders march up to the battle area—France, June 1944*

Troops of the Royal Scots Fusiliers wait in an orchard for the advance while a barrage is laid down—near Tilley, 26 June 1944*

The 2nd Gordons outside a German bunker, captured with ninety prisoners, February 1945*

[xii]

Men of the Royal Scots after clearing the Japanese out of Payan, January 1945*

A ceremonial parade of the Royal Scots Fusiliers led by the pipe band, at Tananarive, Madagascar*

Inscription on a rock in Dongala Gorge, Somalia ('*Soldier*' *magazine*)

Cameronians at church parade ('*Soldier*' *magazine*)

The scene after the Battle of the Hook, Korea*

* *Photographs supplied by the Imperial War Museum*

I

'The Wild and Savage Scots'

SOMETIMES OLD battlefields fail to stir the imagination, perhaps because Nature and Man have made such drastic changes that even a knowledgeable and sensitive person cannot re-create, in his mind's eye, the battles of yesterday.

I have soaked myself, more than most people, in the atmosphere of battlefields and I can now walk over some of them without my palms becoming moist and a lump coming to my throat. Others do not move me as much on a second visit as they did on the first.

But there is one battlefield and one spot on that battlefield that will always stir me. The battlefield is Tobruk and the spot is a few miles outside the town, where now stands a cairn, a monument to the Black Watch.

Now, Tobruk, historically and militarily, may be legitimately regarded as Australian property, but that lonely cairn on the Bardia road and the area around it, where men of the Black Watch fought and died, is holy Scottish soil and it moves me deeply. It is not far from Tobruk War Cemetery, where Scots, among others, are buried.

I remember the first time I saw that cairn. I was driving across the desert to Tobruk, driving through a mist of memories. And I was despondent because this was a lonely battlefield, abandoned to the Bedouins and the sun, and so very few people would ever see it. Here men had fought and bled and died—here, away, far away, from home.

Then I saw the cairn, formed of rough-hewn stone, upthrust against the flat, hard desert. I stopped the truck, walked the few paces to the cairn and read the inscription:

In memory
of those gallant officers and men of
the
2nd Bn. The Black Watch
who fell in this area on
21st Nov. 1941
in the attack from the Tobruk Defences

Scots. Highlanders. Jocks. What bitter mockery it was for a Scot of all people to die in a waterless, grassless desert, away from his hills and glens.

But then, I thought, Highlanders for centuries had been dying violently away from home—on the plains of Spain, in the passes of the Pyrenees, in the arid heat or stinging cold of northern India, at the Khyber Pass, at Lucknow, Omdurman, Tel-el-Kebir, Alma, Inkermann, Balaklava—hundreds of places in jungle, mountain and desert—renowned battles and minor campaigns remembered now by nobody other than the sensitive men who collect medals issued for those campaigns and fights. In a dozen countries memorials in lonely places showed that the Scots had passed that way. I had seen some of those memorials —the one on the hill at Magersfontein, a Celtic cross in grey granite, twenty feet high, with this inscription:

Erected by Scots the world over in memory of the officers and men of the Highland regiments who fell at Magersfontein, December 11, 1899.

Scotland is poorer in men
but richer in heroes

And the simple but eloquent one at Kohima, Burma, to the 1st Camerons and the even plainer one at Keren, where, set into the rocks at the foot of Dongala Gorge, are the words 'H.L.I. Scotland for Ever'.

Famous in their time, all these places are off the map and the memorials, sadly, have nobody to inspire.

The sun was high and moisture trickled down my face. The air shimmered above the barren ground and the quietness was oddly disturbing. Silence and solitude *here*, where once there had been a very hell of noise, where men of half a dozen races had panted and sweated in the sun.

Then, muffled through the haze, I heard the pipes. They were in my mind, of course; I heard them because I wanted to hear them, because here, around me, Black Watch men had died. The pipes were playing a lament; it sounded like the 'Land o' the Leal'.

I walked out into the desert, finding the still, small debris of battle—cartridge cases, a boot heel, a piece of belt buckle, a bullet-shattered water bottle, a dented tin hat without its lining. All these things had once belonged to men. The men were gone, some of them for ever, but their relics remained, more enduring than flesh.

After a time I returned to my truck—a War Graves Commission vehicle which was giving me a lift to Tobruk—but I found it difficult to leave that cairn. I was tremendously impressed that the regiment should want to build it—to keep alive the memory of comrades, to build it *here*, knowing that nobody would ever see it. This impressed me most of all. Scottish clannishness.

The Scots are different from other people—not in any peculiar way, but distinctively different. They have an innate pride of race, and, militarily, an intense pride of regiment. Not that this is peculiar in the British Army, but somehow the Scots have always been more fiercely aggressive in their traditions.

Over the centuries Scottish soldiers have made a deep impression on many people and it is interesting to read the comments of these people. Some commended, some condemned—but the significant fact is that nobody was ever indifferent. The Scot is too much of an individualist—even when his identity is lost within a regiment—to be treated with indifference.

* * *

Scottish regiments—and Highland ones in particular—owe much of their character to the way in which chiefs disciplined and trained all the men of their clans, long before regiments, as such, were thought of. A chief had absolute power and between him and every member of his clan was complete confidence and devotion. It was so complete, in fact, that its depth is difficult to appreciate today.

Severe punishment was seldom necessary. Death was reserved for traitors or for murder within the clan. A chief could inflict one punishment almost as terrifying as death— banishment from the clan. This was a serious matter, for a man without a clan was a man without a friend and once banished he would find it very difficult to persuade another chief to accept him.

When the MacGregors lost their lands, at a time when even the use of their name was illegal, no less a man than Rob Roy was forced to seek protection from the Campbell chief.

Clanship and brotherhood were always fostered. One custom was for the chief to entrust his heir to some chosen clansman for a few years. The clansman's children and the chief's heir grew up together more or less as foster brothers and sisters, devotedly loyal for the rest of their lives.

Once, when some men of one clan had disgraced themselves in battle, the chief mustered his entire clan. Each offender was then called out and ordered to touch his tongue with his fingers and cry out, in Gaelic, 'This is the coward who fled!' To a proud Scot this was a bitter punishment indeed.

Clansmen were given what amounted to commando training, with emphasis on fieldcraft and handling of weapons rather than on drill. In hunting wolves and foxes and in stealing cattle they were learning many valuable military lessons. The Camerons and MacDonells of Keppoch raided as far afield as Nairn and Moray. The MacPhersons, MacBeans, Frasers, MacGillivrays and Mackintoshes all suffered at the hands of the Camerons and MacDonells.

Some clans, like the Macleods, Macleans, MacNeils and MacDonalds had their own private navies operating on the west coast and among the Western Isles. At least once a year, usually between sowing and harvest, most clans carried out a *tainchel* or deer drive, which was semi-military in character and which involved military-style manoeuvres. A *tainchel* was highly organized and strictly controlled and the men lived off the land while it lasted. When they had a day off they engaged in sports and games and from these developed the Highland Games as we know them today.

As far back as the year 1250 Bartholomew, an Englishman, was writing: 'The londe Scotia hath the name of Scottes that there dwelle. The men are lygthe of harte, fiers and couragious on theyr enmyes. They love nyghe as well death as thraldome, and they account it for slouth to dye in bed, and a great wor- shyppe and vertue to deye in a felde fyghtynge agynst enmyes.'

At this time Scotsmen were already protecting the French kings and for three or four centuries later the 'Scottish Guard' was famed for its devotion.

About 1500 a Venetian traveller wrote about the Scots in his *A Relation of the Isle of England*:

The inhabitants of the country [the Highlands] are called the wild and savage Scots, not, however, from the rudeness of their manners which are extremely courteous. . . . These savages are great soldiers, and when they go to war, the privilege of guarding the King's person belongs to them.

Don Peter [de Ayala, Spanish Ambassador to Scotland] also says that all the Scotch nation are extremely partial to foreigners, and very hospitable, and that they all consider that there is no higher duty in the world than to love and defend their crown. And that whenever the King is pleased to go to war he can raise, without any prejudice to the country, 50,000 or 60,000 men, who, being suddenly called together with their rich and handsome equipments, serve at their own expense for the space of 30 days and if the war should continue beyond that time they are dismissed, having previously been replaced by a force of equal magnitude. Any who are not summoned to take part in the war would feel themselves to be slighted and under the displeasure of the King. . . . Don Peter himself told me that he had seen them several times in the field and that he never saw anything better appointed.

The historian Froissart speaks of the Scots as bold, hardy and much inured to war in a national sense and Stocqueler records that 'From the days of Louis XI of France to the 30 years War —1617–1648—the valour, coolness and probity of the Scottish Soldier continued to rise to higher and higher estimation in every country in which he took service'.

Actually, the historian was doing the Scots rather an in- justice, as they had been prominent in France for long before 1617. Some French writers refer to Scots in French military service as early as 1380, during the reign of Henry V.

King Louis XII wrote: 'The institution of the Scots Men-at- Arms and the Scots Lifeguards was an acknowledgement of the service the Scots rendered to Charles VII in reducing France to his obedience, and of the great loyalty and virtue which he found in them.'

According to General Susanne, in his *Histoire de la Cavalerie*, Les Gendarmes Ecossais (or La Garde Ecossaise du Corps du Roi) was brought into France in 1422 and was known under this title right up till 1788.

In 1425 we find in the *Registres de la Chambre des Comptes* the first mention of a Scottish company of 'men-at-arms and archers ordonnéz à la garde du corps du roi under the command of Christin Chambre of Scotland . . . by letters of 8th July, 1425'. Probably this date should be given as the foundation of the Scots bodyguard, definitely organized in 1445. But from 1425 the kings of France were guarded by Scotsmen, who for nearly 300 years served France with unswerving fidelity.

Scottish soldiers fought for Joan of Arc at Jargeau, Patay, Orleans and other battles. In 1430 Joan went to Lagny-sur-Marne, where she knew to be 'men who made good war against the English'. They were Scottish troops commanded by Sir Hugh Kennedy, who had already fought for her at Orleans and Patay. With Kennedy's men Joan cut to pieces an English force near Lagny; it was her last exploit before capture.

Whenever Charles VII captured a city he was escorted into it by the Scots Guards 'more gorgeously clad than the rest'. They wore jackets without sleeves, red, white and green, covered with gold embroidery, with plumes in their helms of the same colours and their swords and leg-harness richly mounted in silver.

Louis XI had such faith in the Scots Guards that on his death-bed he entrusted to them the care of his son, Charles VIII.

Had there been newspapers in those days the Scots often would have been in the news. An Italian writer, Giornali Passero, noted 'that the Scots archers were real giants, for the shortest of them stood nine hands high; no finer troop could be seen'.

When Charles VIII was in Rome in 1494 his Scots attracted much attention. There, as elsewhere, they guarded not only the first door, but all the doors giving access to the king's lodgings.

When Charles died at the age of twenty-nine two of the Scots actually died of grief; this is clearly stated in the *Registres du Parlement*, a French official record.

Louis XII, in consideration of the great services rendered to France by Scotland, especially in the war against England, exempted all Scots resident in France from the obligation of asking for letters of naturalization, granting to them universally the privileges of making wills or succeeding to inheritance by intestacy, and of holding public offices and benefices, as if they had been French by birth. This privilege was added to by several later French kings.

In 1515 when Louis XII was dying, he made Marshal Stewart of Aubigny and his lieutenant, John Stewart, swear on the Gospel that they would execute the terms of his will. Stewart swore that he and his hundred archers would do so, or lose their lives.

Claude Seyssel, one of the great dignitaries of Louis XII's court, has left a fine testimony of the regard in which the Scots Guards were held. 'For so long a time as they have served in France, never hath there been one of them that hath committed any fault against the kings or their own subjects.'

In his turn Louis XIV maintained the companies of Scots Men-at-Arms and Scots Guards, the only two corps in the French Army which had survived the troubles of the sixteenth century, and allowed both companies to remain in possession of their privileges. The Guards took precedence of the whole French Army by virtue of seniority. The Men-at-Arms became the first cavalry corps in France after the Royal Household Cavalry.

It became such a great honour to enter the Guards or the Men-at-Arms that after 1666 Frenchmen were permitted to enter, although from time to time descendents of the first Scottish soldiers were admitted.

Minden in August 1759 was the last battlefield of the Scots Men-at-Arms. General Susanne wrote: 'The Scotch company of men-at-arms affords an unparalleled example in European military annals of a corps lasting uninterruptedly for 360 years without material transformation as to organization, attributes and military service. Under the title of Scots Men-at-Arms [Gens d'Armes Ecossais] one might write the history of the wars waged by France from the days of Joan of Arc to the Revolution.'

The Scots Guards were at the head of the French Army in all the great battles fought under Louis XIV. In 1709, at Malplaquet, with Prince James Stewart at their head, they pierced four lines of the enemy. The Battle of Lawfeld in 1747 was the last in which the Scots Guards were engaged, and by this time, as with the Men-at-Arms, many of the guardsmen were French.

Other Scottish regiments were formed in France by the thousands of Jacobites who came to France. The units included the Hamilton, Campbell, Royal Ecossais, Ogilvy, Douglas and Albany regiments. Most had a short life.

The Royal Ecossais was typical. Raised on 1 August 1744, by Louis Drummond, Duke of Perth, it took part in the Battle of Fontenoy, the capture of Tourney, Oudenarde, Ghent and Nieuport; sailed to Scotland on 26 November 1745 and took part in the Battle of Culloden. The colonel was mortally wounded and was succeeded by Louis Drummond, Earl of Melfort. On its return to France, the regiment formed part of the army of Flanders in 1748 and took part in the siege of Maestricht, the defence of Marburg, and the Battle of Willingshausen, 1761. In 1762 it was incorporated with another regiment.

In 1815, with the restoration of the French monarchy, Louis XVIII reinstated the French Scots Guards, but they disappeared—this time forever—with the revolution of 1830.

The Scots in French service were frankly mercenary and not ashamed of it. Fighting was in their blood and they regarded it as naturally as they did eating. But more than this, these Scots fought in order to eat. The Highlanders sent expeditions to rob the Lowlanders or even other hostile Highland clans, while the Lowlanders, in turn, raided the English over the border. These expeditions were not always successful and when times were hard the Scots looked around for something they could sell. All they had to offer was their fighting ability—and this they sold to Continental armies, not only to the French, but to the Swedes and the Germans, among others.

But unlike most mercenaries the Scots were loyal to their salt and there is no recorded instance of their having failed their foreign masters. They took their job seriously and were highly regarded everywhere.

Writing of Scottish troops in 1633, Daniel Defoe said:

I observed that these parties had always some foot with them and yet if the horse galloped, or pushed on ever so forward, the foot was as forward as they, which was an extraordinary advantage. Gustavus Adolphus, the king of soldiers, was the first that ever I observed who found the advantage of mixing small bodies of musquetters among his horse, and had he had such nimble strong fellows as these, he could have proved them above all the rest of his men.

These were those they call Highlanders; they would run on foot with their arms, and all their accoutrements, and keep very good order too, and yet keep pace with the horses, let them go at what rate they would. . . . I confess the soldiers made a very uncouth figure, especially the Highlanders, the oddness and barbarity of their arms seemed to have in it something remarkable. They were generally tall swinging fellows; their swords were extravagantly, and I think insignificantly broad, and they carried great wooden targets, large enough to cover the upper parts of their bodies. Their dress was as antique as the rest; a cap on their heads, called by them a bonnet, long hanging sleeves behind, and their doublets, breeches, and stockings of a stuff they call plaid, stripes across red and yellow, with short cloaks of the same. There were three or four thousand of them . . . armed only with swords and targets; and in their belts some of them had a pistol, but no muskets at that time amongst them.

The Scots could use their weapons, too, and their training was thorough.

Early in the seventeenth century the chief of the Frasers spent several months each year at Stratherrick, training his men in shooting bow and gun and giving them all kinds of exercises designed to make them fit and tough.

Just how tough the Scots were at this period is exemplified by Sir Ewen Cameron of Lochiel, who, at sixty, fought on foot at the Battle of Killiecrankie. At twenty-five he had spent a year harassing the English garrison at Inverlochy. The English sent a large armed party to cut down his woods; Cameron attacked them and killed 138 English, though his own force was only a quarter the strength of the English.

Lochiel closed with the English commander and together they rolled into a ditch. Weaponless, Lochiel bit his enemy's throat 'quitt throw' and killed him. Soon after this happened, Lochiel's foster-brother saw an English soldier about to shoot his chief at close range; he ran in front of Locheil and was killed by the shot. It was inevitable that Lochiel would kill the English soldier personally.

Probably it was about the time of Killiecrankie that he reproached one of his sons for using a snowball as a pillow during a winter bivouac; this was an effeminate practice, the Chief said caustically. His spartan life in no way affected Lochiel's health. He died in 1718 at the age of eighty-nine.

I

Pitt and the Highlanders

DURING THE first quarter of the eighteenth century there were no Highlanders in the British Army, but some Lowland regiments had been serving for nearly a hundred years. The Lowland regiments were: the Royal Scots, Royal Scots Greys, Scots Guards, Royal Scots Fusiliers, King's Own Scottish Borderers and the Cameronians.* All were fine, vigorous and colourful troops but as yet they had no integration whatever with the Highlanders. In fact, the Highlanders were often in bitter conflict with Lowland soldiers serving with the British Army.

In 1724, an English observer wrote: 'The Highlanders are a source of detestation to their Lowland countrymen and are viewed by the English as veritable savages, even as cannibals. English officers deem service along their frontier as a perilous and profitless exile, as the legionaries of Rome did their campaigns in Britain.'

In view of this outlook it is necessary here to appreciate the circumstances which brought the Highlanders into English service—a remarkable achievement considering that they had fought the English and their Lowland soldiers for so very long.

In 1725 the government passed the Disarming Act, designed to cool the martial fire of the Highlanders and to weaken the clan system. General Wade was given the task of implementing the Act and ordered to build 450 miles of new roads and a number of forts. The idea was to be able to move troops rapidly to any flare-up. Some of his companies wore a dark tartan and were nicknamed *am Freicaeden Dubh* (Black Watch)

* All dealt with in separate chapters.

in contrast to *Saighdearan Dearg* (Red Soldiers), the regulars in their scarlet tunics.

These units were known as Independent Companies because they operated only in the district in which they were raised. It was a good system because the men knew the district intimately and were themselves known and, mostly, respected. Discipline was hardly on English Army lines; many private soldiers in the Companies had batmen of their own and there was no social discrimination between officers and men.

In 1739 the older Companies, with four new ones, were amalgamated into a regiment, known then as the 43rd or Highland Regiment of Foot. It mustered as a regiment for the first time the following year and was the first Highland regiment. It certainly started something.

But before any more development could occur there was the tragedy of the '45 Rebellion, which was largely a matter of Scot fighting Scot and, on at least one occasion, Highlander fighting Highlander. When it was all over somebody—many people give the credit to William Pitt*—realized that Highlanders would make fine troops.

The English had learned the hard way that a Highland charge was one of the most terrifying of war experiences. These physically tough and morally righteous men from the hills were virtually invincible and could put the fear of the devil into most of their enemies. Only the most experienced and disciplined troops could stand up to them.

What Highland initiative and enterprise could do was well shown at the Battle of Prestonpans in September 1745. The English force, under Sir John Cope, thought they were safe because there was a morass between them and the Scots. But during the night the Scots, three abreast, crossed the marsh in silence and then charged with pistol and claymore into the English camp. The Guards tried to stop the rush but were swept away. In a few minutes the Highlanders had captured the artillery, stores and money-chest of Cope's army. For years

* In a famous speech before Parliament in 1766 Pitt said: 'I sought for merit where it was to be found . . . and found it in the mountains of the north. I called it forth and drew into your service a hardy and intrepid race of men, who when left by your jealousy became a prey to the artifice of your enemies, and had gone nigh to have overturned the State. . . . These men were brought to combat on your side; they served with fidelity as they fought with valour, and conquered for you in every part of the world.'

afterwards the pipers of Highland regiments in the British Army played a tune called 'Hey, Johnny Cope, are ye wauken yet?'

The little kilted army began its march on London, but three strong forces soon began to threaten it. Charles Edward turned back at Derby and reached Scotland in safety. The Duke of Cumberland, 'the Butcher', leading 10,000 disciplined troops, caught the remnants of the Highland Army at Culloden Moor and destroyed them.

The bitterness after the '45 subsided only slowly, for the government was determined now to wipe out the clan system and this it did, for all practical purposes. The end result was probably a good one, for all Scotland became one big clan eventually and many old enmities disappeared.

The news of General Burgoyne's disaster at Saratoga, in 1777 (during the War of American Independence) stirred up Scottish patriotism. The Duke of Hamilton, chief of Scotland's peers, raised a regiment of 1000 men on his own estate, and went with it to America as a captain. Another peer, the Duke of Atholl, also enlisted a regiment from among his retainers, which fought in many battles before being disbanded. He not only gave two guineas to each recruit as a bounty, but he also supported the various families which the 'absent-minded beggars' of those times left behind. Chief Macleod, who had formerly been a strong supporter of Prince Charlie, also founded a regiment, which afterwards became the 1st Highland Light Infantry. The cities of Edinburgh and Glasgow each raised and equipped a regiment, as did the families of Argyll, Gordon, Seaforth, and Macdonald; but nearly all these, after they had done their work in America, were disbanded. That recruited by the Earl of Seaforth, however, was retained in the service, and it is now the 1st Seaforth Highlanders.

This was typical of the way, rather by fits and starts, in which the Highland soldier became a permanent part of the British Army.

Gradually other Highland regiments were formed. The last regular one, the 93rd Sutherland Highlanders (later the 2nd Argyll and Sutherland Highlanders) appeared on the scene in 1800.

By then Britain had good reason to be glad of her Highland

troops and her Scottish regiments generally; they had already seen a lot of action in many theatres of war. So serious was England's position at this time—the last quarter of the eighteenth century—that her history might well be different had not the Highlanders joined the colours.

Between 1740 and 1815 no fewer than fifty battalions of the line, three of reserve and seven of militia were raised in the Highlands, in addition to twenty-six regiments of fencibles— regular troops embodied for the duration of a war. There were other volunteer and local militia units. The Lowlands raised only a few less battalions.

Before the century was over an Austrian wrote this of the Highland soldier: 'The Scottish Highlanders are a people totally different in their dress, manners and temperament from the other inhabitants of Britain . . . as they are strangers to fear, they make very fine soldiers when disciplined. . . . The French had first held them in contempt, but they have met them so often in recent years and seen them in the front of so many battles that they now firmly believe that the British Army is mostly Scottish.'

Later, Wellington, too, had a fine appreciation of his Scottish troops. In his Waterloo dispatch he mentioned only four regiments and three of them were Scottish—Black Watch, Camerons and Gordons.

After Waterloo the British wounded were very well treated by the Belgians, who admired the troops' stoical endurance. The hardihood of the Scots particularly impressed the Belgians. One woman, who was housing several soldiers, told Sir Walter Scott that his countrymen were made of iron, not flesh and blood.

'I saw a wounded Highlander stagger along the street,' she said, 'supporting himself on the fence rails. I approached him and said, "I'm afraid you are severely hurt."

' "I was born in Lochaber,"* the soldier answered dis- dainfully, "and I do not care much for a wound." '

But before the woman could call for help to get the man to her house he collapsed at her feet, dying.

Another observer recorded that in Antwerp much was said of the Highlanders:

* He was probably a Cameron Highlander.

A gentleman had, when the wounded arrived, been recognized and spoken to by a poor Highlander. The circumstance absolutely gave him a kind of consideration in the crowd; he felt prouder at that moment than if a prince had smiled upon him. At Brussels, and everywhere in the Netherlands, when the English troops were mentioned, whom they likewise much admired, the natives always returned to the Scotch with 'But the Scots, they were good and kind, as well as brave; they are the only soldiers who become members of the family in the houses in which they are billeted; they even carry about the children and do the domestic work'. The favourite proverbial form of compliment was, 'Lions in the field and lambs in the house'.

There was a competition among the inhabitants who should have them in their houses; and when they returned wounded, the same house they had left had its doors open, and the family went out some miles to meet 'our own Scotsman'. The people had many instances to relate of the generosity of these men; after the battle many, although themselves wounded, were seen binding up the wounds of the French and assisting them with their arm. On the contrary, it is well known that very few of our soldiers fell into the hands of the enemy, without being murdered in cold blood. There cannot be a better test of two nations, a more satisfactory decision of the question on which the peace and happiness of mankind should depend.

Blücher, in a dispatch relating to the Battle of Waterloo, wrote, 'The Old Guard were baffled by the intrepidity of the Scottish regiments'. This account of the conduct of the Highlanders was confirmed by the prevailing belief both in Paris and throughout France. The French soldiers themselves said that it was the Scottish troopers who chiefly occasioned the loss of the battle by defeating the Old Guard. The impression they made in Paris was remarkable. Tartan became a prevailing fashion with the ladies, and the full garb was employed as an attraction by wax-work exhibitors. It was also introduced on the stage with great applause.

Wolseley, speaking of the Highland Brigade in the Crimea—the 42nd (Black Watch), 79th (Camerons) and 93rd (Argylls) said: 'They were the finest brigade I ever saw in any country.' And after the Battle of the Alma, that fine old soldier Colin Campbell asked for permission—and obtained it—to wear a Highland feather bonnet himself as a mark of honour to the Highlanders.

Campbell knew his Highlanders, as he showed at the Alma. Just before the brigade received the order to take the heights on which the enemy was strongly posted, Sir Colin addressed his troops. 'Now, men, you are going into action; remember that where you fall you must lie until the bandsmen pick you up. If any man leaves the ranks to help a wounded comrade I'll post his name on the parish church.' No greater indignity could befall a Highland soldier than to have his name put on the church door of his native place; apart from the shame, the lassies would have nothing to do with him when he returned home. The Highlanders made their charge, and, driving back the Russians, won the heights of Alma.

When leaving his brigade, Sir Colin said: 'Men, remember never to lose sight of the fact that you are natives of Scotland; that your country admires you for your bravery; that it still expects much from you; and, as Scotsmen, strive to maintain the name and fame of your countrymen, who are everywhere, and who have nobly fought and bled in all quarters of the globe.'

Of the 'Saviours of India'—the 78th—Havelock wrote: 'In the whole of my career I have never seen a regiment behave better, nay more, I have never seen any regiment behave so well as the 78th Highlanders [Seaforths] this day [the taking of Cawnpore]. I am not a Highlander, but I wish I were one.'

At the end of the Afghanistan campaign in 1880 Roberts told the Highlanders (72nd and 92nd) with him: 'You beat them at Kabul and you have beaten them at Kandahar and now, as you are about to leave the country, you may be assured that the very last troops the Afghans want to meet are the Scottish Highlanders and the Gurkhas.'

At the Atbara, Kitchener told the colonel of the Camerons: 'What your battalion has done is one of the finest feats performed for many years.'

In 1901 General Smith-Dorrien told them: 'You have done more marching than any other regiment in South Africa, but I have never met a more uncomplaining regiment. . . . From the bottom of my heart I thank you. . . .'

For the Camerons the Battle of Loos in 1915 is a particular epic. Writing of the 5th Battalion, an historian said: 'Nothing but death could stop such men.'

In the House of Commons, Churchill said of the battle: 'One battalion of the Cameron Highlanders went into action 850 strong and the colonel, the adjutant and 110 men who were the survivors, took and held their objectives. Four successive lines were swept away, but the fifth went on without

[16]

hesitation; while, two days later, the remnant were asked to make an attack, and did it with the greatest *élan* and spirit.'

A captured German document paid a tribute to the illustrious 51st Highland Division in 1917. The Scots, the document stated, 'were the most to be feared Division in the whole of the British Army'.

Of the 15th Division, which had five battalions of Highlanders among its nine Scottish infantry battalions, General Dempsey wrote in 1944: 'It was the 15th Scottish Division which broke through the enemy's main defensive line south of Caumont on July 30, and opened the way for the Armoured Divisions. . . . You have set the very highest standard since the day you landed in Normandy and I hope you are as proud of your achievements as I am to have you under my command.'

In more recent years Lord Wavell has said:

The Highlands of Scotland have always been famous for their fighting men. . . . They were formidable warriors indeed, matchless in endurance and courage, unsurpassed for swiftness and vigour in attack. . . . To the fighting qualities of the old stock has been added the steadfast discipline of the regular soldier; and the Highland regiments still remain the finest fighting force in the British Isles, with a record of service which shows that some or other of them have been engaged and have distinguished themselves in practically every campaign of the British Army for the last 200 years. His native stubbornness added to his regular discipline and training has made the Highlander as steadfast in defence as any, but he has always kept the fierceness and swiftness in attack for which his ancestors were so famous.

Wavell, who served in the Black Watch, mentioned also the camaraderie among Highland regiments. 'We have always trusted each other and have been proud and glad to find another Highland regiment alongside, in barracks or on battlefield.' For a Scottish regiment has always fought even better when brigaded with other Scots; then a man *knew* with the utter certainty that the sun would rise that he need not worry about his flanks or about support arriving in time . . . or about anything.

When Dr. Johnson was compiling his dictionary, he said this about oats: 'In Scotland, food for men; in England, for horses.' It is said that he read the uncomplimentary definition to a Scottish friend, and asked him how he liked it. 'Couldn't be better,' was the reply. 'But you might add that there is no food equal to it; for where will you find such horses as in England, and where such men as in Scotland?'

And this, perhaps, is the key to the character of the Scottish soldier—for never has a man been more male, never has a male been more conscious of his vigour, never a soldier more intensely aware of the surge of racial pride, never a being more suffused with clannish fervour, never one filled with such tremendous will.

III

Loyalty and Duty

SIR WALTER SCOTT* in *Quentin Durward* and *The Legend of
Montrose*, sketched the character of his countrymen of these
early periods, but is hardly just in his reflections. 'The contempt of commerce entertained by young men having some
pretence to gentility, the poverty of the country of Scotland,
the national disposition to wandering and to adventure, all
conduced to lead the Scots abroad into the military service of
countries that were at war with each other. They were distinguished on the Continent by their bravery, but in adopting the
trade of mercenary soldiers they necessarily injured their
national character.'

Time has not proved this to be true. In any case, unlike
other mercenaries, the Scots were liked in the countries where
they fought. German mercenaries, while good soldiers as a
rule, were usually detested by everybody including their
temporary comrades-in-arms.

I like what Scott has Quentin Durward say: 'Were I King
Louis, I would trust my safety to the faith of the 300 Scottish
gentlemen, throw down my bounding walls to fill up the moat,
call in my noble peers and paladins, and live as became me,
amid breaking of lances in gallant tournaments, and feasting of

* Scott himself liked soldiering. He served with the Edinburgh Troop of Mid-
lothian Yeomanry Cavalry. Lord Cockburn wrote: 'It was not a duty with him, or a
necessity, nor a pastime, but an absolute passion, indulgence in which gratified his
feudal taste for war and his jovial sociableness. He drilled, and drank, and made
songs with a hearty conscientious earnestness which inspired or shamed everybody
within the attraction. His troop used to practise individually, with the sabre, at a
turnip, which was struck on the top of a staff, to represent a Frenchman, in front of
the line. Sir Walter pricked forward gallantly, saying to himself, "Cut them down, the
villains, cut them down!" and made his blow, which, from his lameness, was often
an awkward one, cordially muttering curses all the while at the detested enemy.'

days with nobles, and have no more fear of a foe than I have of a fly.'

One of the most remarkable of many Scottish officers to serve a foreign master was Marshal Keith, who was in the Russian Army before entering Prussian service. He first distinguished himself in 1737, when he was in the army of Count Munick sent to capture Otchakoff from the Turks. By his valour and skill, Keith, at the head of 8,000 men, contributed greatly to the capture of the place. A humane man, he checked the ferocity of the Muscovite soldiery.

He saw a Cossack about to cut off the head of a seven-year-old girl, and stopped the soldier. The father of the child had been a Turkish pasha of importance. The girl was now an orphan and Keith adopted her; when she grew up she took over the management of his home.

In 1737, Keith represented the Russians at peace talks with the Turks, who were represented by their Grand Vizier. The two men carried on their negotiations through interpreters. When it was all over and informality had set in, the Grand Vizier grasped Keith by the hand and said: 'I'm unco happy to meet a countryman in your exalted station.'

'A countryman?' Keith said. '*You* are a Scot?'

'Dinna be surprised,' the Grand Vizier said. 'I'm o' the same country wi' yoursell, mon. I mind weel seeing you and your brothers, when boys, passin' by to the school at Kirkcaldy. My father was bellman o' Kirkcaldy.'

Keith was killed at the Battle of Hochkirchen in 1758, as he was charging the Austrians for the third time at the head of his Prussian soldiers. Though a thrifty man, Keith had only £35 when he died, so the thought of riches had not taken him into a military career. It could only have been the love of action.

For many years nobody bothered to wonder what motivated a Scot or why he made a good soldier. One of the first people to do so was General Garth Stewart, writing in 1822, particularly about the Highlander:

In 1793, and the succeeding years, the whole strength and resources of the United Empire were called into action. In the northern corner of the kingdom a full proportion of its absolute resources was produced. A couple struggling against the disadvantages of a boisterous climate, and barren soil, could not be expected to contribute money. But the personal services of the young and active were ready for the defence of the liberty and independence of their country. The men whom these districts sent forth, in the hour of danger, possessed that vigour and hardihood peculiar to an agricultural and pastoral life. As a proof of this, in late years, when typhus and other epidemic diseases were prevalent in the south it was so different in the mountains. Except in cases where infection was carried from the low country, few instances of typhus or other contagious distempers occurred, and where they actually broke out, they did not spread, as might naturally have been expected, from the confined and small dwellings of the Highland peasantry. This fact can only be accounted for from their habitual temperance, and that robust vigour of constitution produced by sobriety and exercise.

It may, therefore, be allowed that the effective national defence which the agricultural population afford the state, is to be valued beyond a numerical force of another description, in so far as a man, whose strength of constitution enables him to serve his country, for a term of years, though subjected to privations and changes of climate, is more valuable than the man whose constitution gives way in half the time. This remark applies forcibly in the present instance. Indeed, where sickness has prevailed among Highland soldiers, it has in general been occasioned less by fatigue, privations, or exposure to cold, than from the nature of the provisions, particularly animal food, and from clothing unnecessarily warm.

These were excellent men, healthy, vigorous, and efficient; attached and obedient to their officers, temperate and regular; in short possessing those principles of integrity and moral conduct which constitute a valuable soldier. The duty of officers was easy with such men, who only required to be told what duty was expected of them. A young officer, endowed with sufficient judgment to direct them in the field, possessing energy and spirit to ensure the respect and confidence of soldiers, and prepared, on every occasion, to show them the eye of the enemy, need not desire a command that would sooner, and more permanently, establish his professional character, if employed on an active campaign, than that of 1000 such men.

Among these men desertion was unknown, and corporal punishment unnecessary. The detestation and disgrace of such a mode of punishment would have rendered a man infamous in his own estimation, and an outcast from the society of his country and kindred. Fortunately for these men they were placed under the command of an officer well calculated for the charge. Born among themselves, of a family which they were accustomed to respect, and possessing both judgment and temper, he perfectly understood their character, and ensured their esteem and regard.

Many brave honest soldiers have been lost from the want of such men at their head. The appointment of a commander to a corps, so composed, is a subject of deep importance. The colonel knew his men, and the value which they attached to a good name, by tarnishing which they would bring shame on their country and kindred. In case of an misconduct, he had only to remonstrate or threaten to transmit to their parents a report of their misbehaviour. This was, indeed, to them a grievous punishment, acting like the curse of Kehama, as a perpetual banishment from a country to which they could not return with a bad character. For several years during which Colonel Mackenzie commanded the Seaforths, he seldom had occasion to resort to any other restraint.

The same system was followed up with such success by his immediate successors, Lieutenant-Colonels Mackenzie and Adams, that, after being many years in India, very little change occurred in the behaviour of the men, except that they had become more addicted to liquor than formerly. Selling regimental necessaries, or disorderly conduct in barracks, were very uncommon, and the higher crimes totally unknown. They were steady and economical, lived much among themselves, seldom mixed with other corps, were much attached to many of their officers, and extremely national.

And national Scots have remained. After the surrender of Lord Cornwallis's army in America in 1781, the 75th was marched in detachments as prisoners to different parts of Virginia. Here they met many of their emigrant countrymen and Americans, who used 'every endeavour and made many tempting offers' to induce the soldiers to break their allegiance and become subjects of the American government. Yet not a single Highlander allowed himself to be seduced by their offers.

When it was known in Sutherland in 1793, on the breaking out of the war with revolutionary France, that the Countess of Sutherland was expected to call forth some of the most able-bodied men on her extensive estates, the officers whom she appointed had only to make a selection of those who were best calculated to fill up the ranks of the regiment. Enlistment was completed in as short a time as the men could be collected from their rugged and distant districts. For five years after the regiment—the 93rd, later the Argyll and Sutherland High-landers—was formed not an individual in it committed a crime of any kind. During the rebellion in Ireland, in 1797–8, 'their conduct and manners so softened the horrors of war that they were not a week in any fresh quarter or cantonment without conciliating and becoming intimate with the people'.

In 1800 the regiment had been nineteen years without a punishment parade.

General Stewart said:

The sense of duty is not extinguished in the Highland soldier by absence from the mountains. It accompanies him amid the dissipations of a mode of life to which he has not been accustomed. It prompts him to save a portion of his pay to enable him to assist his parents, and also to work when he has an opportunity, that he may increase their allowance; at once preserving himself from idle habits and contributing to the happiness and comfort of those who gave him birth. Filial attachment is a strong principle with the Highlander, and it has generally been found that a threat of informing their parents of misconduct has operated as a sufficient check on young soldiers, who always receive the intimation with a sort of horror.

The Scots anticipated by centuries the relationship between officers and men which was to become such an important aspect of the British Army. In the early seventeenth century Colonel Robert Monro raised a regiment, called Mac-Keyes Regiment. Later he wrote a book—*Monro, His Expedition With the Worthy Scots Regiment*—about his experiences with this unit in Swedish service. This extract is significant:

I cannot pass over with silence the love that ordinarily is seen betwixt officers and their followers; being once put under good discipline they will undergo anything for love of their Commanders and Leaders, who have taken pains and diligence in exercising them in perfect use of their arms and in leading them bravely . . . in making with exercise their bodies strong and their hearts valiant. I say, what will they not undertake for the love of their leaders? Truly, they will stand a thousand times more in awe to incur their officers' wrath than through fear of punishment. If they love and respect their officers for their officers' credit they will march so orderly with arms that you would think a whole regiment well disciplined, as this was, that they were all but one body and of one notion, their ears obeying the command all as one, their eyes turning all alike at the first sign given, their hands going to execution as one hand. Their enemies in all encounters could not but duly praise them, calling them the Invincible Old Regiment.

Affection for officers has often been evident. In June 1805 when the 78th (Seaforths) were at Hythe, a field-officer and four subalterns were ordered to join the 1st Battalion in India. The day before the field-officer was to leave the regiment the troops held conferences in barracks and that evening several deputations were sent to him, asking him to apply to remain with the regiment or to take the men with him. But the officer said that he could not refuse his duty.

Next evening when he went into Hythe to take the coach to London about two-thirds of the regiment and a large number of officers accompanied him—all complaining about his departure. The men crowded around the coach and held it up for more than an hour; they clung to the wheels, harness, coach doors and horses, until eventually, the coachman forced his coach through the mass of men, all of whom were crying. The incident was reported to General Sir John Moore and it appealed to him immensely. He took the matter to the commander-in-chief and suggested that the officer be allowed to return to the battalion. This was done and everybody was happy.

This affection has never waned. More than a century later it was noticed in France. In March 1918 a South African officer one night passed four men of the 2nd Royal Scots carrying a dead officer on an improvised bier, made from a length of duckboarding. The moon shone full on the dead man's face and the South African saw that it was Captain Newlands, whom he knew very well. He asked the men where they were carrying the body to.

'No bloody Boche is going to bury our skipper!' one of them said savagely.

They had taken upon themselves the self-imposed task of carrying their company commander back to the next line of defence to ensure him against alien burial.

At one time during the War of American Independence some men of the Black Watch did some officer-carrying under rather different circumstances. The officer was Major Murray, described as 'very corpulent'. Despite his girth, Murray was a soldier, so much so that when attacked by three Americans in a skirmish in 1776 and could not reach his dirk, which had slipped behind his back, he defended himself as well as he could with his fusil, then grabbed the sword of one of his opponents and chased the three Americans off. Later the 42nd under Murray was attacking Fort Washington, situated at the top of a very steep hill. The Highlanders were half-way up the mountain, scaling it like mountain cats, when they heard Murray shout: 'Oh, soldiers, will you leave me?' He stood at the foot of the cliff, unable even to get started and looking upwards hopefully. A party of men went down for him and carried him from ledge to ledge until they reached the summit. They drove the Americans out and captured 200 prisoners—and probably fought all the better for their major's presence.

At Quatre-Bras, two days before Waterloo, a major of the 42nd Highlanders, preferring to fight on foot* in front of his

* In those days infantry officers were mounted.

[24]

men, told a drummer-boy to mind his horse. After some severe fighting with the French cuirassiers and lancers the major was seriously wounded several times and at last fell down from sheer loss of blood. Near him was a private of the regiment, Donald Mackintosh, who was mortally wounded.

The little drummer, seeing his officer fall, ran to his aid. A French lancer made a dash for the fine horse. The wounded Mackintosh, staggering to his feet, said: 'Hoots mon, ye mauna tak that beast; it belongs to our major.'

The Frenchman grabbed the horse's reins, so Donald shot the man out of his saddle; then he died. The major, despite sixteen severe wounds, survived the battle and lived for many years afterwards.

Not everybody understood the Scots. After Torres Vedras, during the Peninsular War, the 94th Brigade (Highlanders) moved to the village of Alcoentre. Unfortunately the English general commanding the brigade was in the same village and he had a great antipathy towards everything Scottish.

Sergeant Donaldson wrote:*

Perhaps he believed, with many people in England, that the Scots run wild about their native hills, eating raw oats like horses, with nothing but a kilt to cover their nakedness, and that they had no right to receive any treatment, when they entered the army, other than that given to any wild animal. Rousing us with a long pole seemed to be his hobby. When our guard turned out to salute him and made some error he would order the sergeant to drill them for an hour, while he stood by and spat 'Scottish savages . . . stupid . . . barbarous'.

At one time on the Peninsula, men of the 94th Brigade found a wine store and plundered it; inevitably some of them became very drunk. The following Sunday, after the chaplain had finished with the church parade, General Picton took his place. Sergeant Donaldson recorded:

This was the first time he had addressed us. I felt anxious to examine the features of a man who had been so much the public talk on account of his reputed cruelty in Trinidad. I could not deny that I felt a prejudice against him and his countenance did not do it away. It had a stern and gloomy expression which, added to a very dark complexion, made it in no way prepossessing.

He opened his mouth and began to pour forth a torrent of abuse on us for

* In *The Eventful Life of a Soldier* (1847).

[25]

our conduct, his dark eyes flashing with indignation as he recapitulated our errors. He wound up his speech with 'You are a disgrace to Scotland'. That had more weight than all his speech. It sank deep in our hearts. To separate a Scotsman from his country—to tell him he is unworthy of it—is next to taking away his life.

IV

Martial Humour

OF ALL soldiers, the Scot probably can be the most homesick, but it would take more than homesickness to impair his fighting qualities, his clear thinking and his sense of humour. A Highlander's initiative never deserts him, as Private Macpherson of the Black Watch proved. In 1764 some of the Black Watch were captured by Red Indians, who tortured the Scots singly before killing them; Macpherson was the last on the list. He didn't mind dying, but did not intend to be tortured. He somehow induced the Indians to believe that he had a secret which would make a warrior impervious to a blow from the sharpest tomahawk and offered himself as a subject for experiment.

He was taken into the forest, where he collected some herbs, mixed their juices and smeared them around his neck. He beckoned to an Indian brave, tried the warrior's blade with his thumb, nodded approval and then laid his head on the block, and invited the brave to try his luck. The Indian struck with such force that he cut the Highlander's head clean off and sent it flying. The Indians, according to the Frenchman who witnessed the incident, were furious at having been tricked out of their torture. It was a neat, grim ruse on the Highlander's part and even to avoid torture it must have taken a lot of courage.

It has always taken something pretty drastic to put a Scot right out of action. In a brush with American rebels in 1777, Sergeant Macgregor of the Black Watch was severely wounded and lay unconscious on the ground. The sergeant was a dandy and was dressed as if going to a ball instead of a battle—new jacket with silver lace, large silver buckles on his shoes and an expensive watch. An American soldier, hungry for loot, slung Macgregor on his back and started off for his own lines, where he could strip the Scot at leisure.

The motion brought Macgregor to and despite his pain, he drew his dirk and grabbed the American's throat with his other hand. 'Tak me hame,' he said, 'or I'll stab ye to the heart.'

The American saw the force of the argument and retraced his steps. Near the British camp they met Lord Cornwallis, who—presumably with a twinkle in his eye—gave the American his liberty for this 'humanity'. His Lordship took a liking to Macgregor, too, and after the sergeant retired found him a job in the Customs House at Leith.

The Highlander, raw from his native hills, was often an innocent, naïve being. Donaldson describes an incident involving the five o'clock breakfast eaten by the men before reporting for working parties. The breakfast was coffee with bread. Donaldson wrote:

I remember the first time we had this sort of breakfast. Each man came forward with his mess-tin for his allowance, which was measured out by the cook. When Donald came up for his issue the cook was carefully skimming the coffee off from the top to avoid stirring up the grounds.

Donald, who thought this was the cook's scheme to keep all the good part to himself, exclaimed: 'Tam your plod! Will you no gie some o' the sik as well as the sin?'

'Certainly,' the cook said. He gave Donald a double ladle of grounds, and Donald came to eat with us, chuckling with satisfaction at having detected the knavery of the cook. 'If she'll socht to sheat a Highlandman, she'll be far mistook,' he said, and broke bread in his coffee, as his comrades were doing.

By this time everyone in the tent was looking at him. Donald began to sup it up with his spoon, but after three mouthfuls, grinding the coffee grounds between his teeth, he threw the tin and all out of the tent. 'Tam their coffee!' he said. 'You might as weel chow leather and drink pog water as that teevil's stuff! Gi'e Donal a cog o' brochan before ony o' your coffees or teas either.'

While serving abroad most Scots thought long and often about home, for the Scot is a sentimentalist. While serving on the Peninsula, Scots of the 94th Brigade were camped one November above the village of Zaggaramurdi, in the Pyrenees.

From a peak above their camp they could see the sea and the towns along the coast. This was the first time in three years that they had the sea in sight, and it moved them deeply. One of them wrote:

A few of us who were drawn together by congeniality of sentiment and disposition used to wander up the giant cliffs and from a vantage point sit and gaze at the ocean and the ships passing, with emotions which I cannot describe. Its expansive bosom seemed a magic mirror wherein we could read our fortune—a happy return from all our dangers, smiling friends, with all the loved associations of childhood and youth swam before our hope-dazzled imaginations and we saw and sang the songs of Scotland while the tears trickled down our cheeks. He who has never heard the melodies of his native land sung in a foreign country is ignorant of a pleasure that nothing can surpass.

Sergeant Forbes Mitchell, of the 93rd, was fond of relating what he called 'a rather laughable incident' concerning a man named Johnny Ross of his company.

Before falling in for the assault on the Begum's palace, during the Indian Mutiny, Ross and George Pullar and some others had been playing cards in a corner and had quarrelled. They were still arguing when the order to fall in was given and Pullar told Ross to shut up. At that moment a spent ball hit Ross in the mouth and knocked out four of his teeth. Ross thought Pullar had punched him and returned the blow.

'You damn fool!' Pullar shouted. 'I didna hit ye! Ye've a bullet in your mouth!'

Ross spat out four teeth and the bullet. 'How the deil can I bite ma cartridges noo?' he said plaintively. Two minutes later he was in action with the bayonet.

At one time, in the Boer War, the Gordons, with fixed bayonets, scaled a kopje only to find that most of the Boers had withdrawn. One Boer, however, was cut off. A Highlander was making for him at the run, when a more athletic comrade passed, shouting, 'Oot o' the way, Jock, and gi'e me room tae get a poke at him'.

'Na, na, Tam', said Jock indignantly. 'Awa' wi' ye and find a Boer tae yoursel'.'

On another occasion the Gordons were briskly engaged, with bullets flying thickly, when one Scot bawled to his mate in front of him, 'Dinna bob, Geordie! I'm ahint ye!'

Toughness and endurance were basically the Scot's stock-in-trade. And he could be tough in more ways than one. During the Boer War, the Modder River at Poplar Grove was for some months a sewer of dead horses, dead men and enteric germs.

One day a Scot and a Tommy bathed in the river. The Scot then filled his water bottle from the river. The Tommy said: 'Why, Jock, boy, there's any amount of good water, well-water, up there.' And he jerked his thumb in the direction of the water-point.

'Na, na, this has mair of a bite', the Highlander said.

A happy character of a later war was Corporal Charlie of the 1/2nd Highland Field Ambulance. At the Battle of Beaumont-Hamel, in November 1916, the corporal was in command of German prisoners being used as bearers. His management of them and of his language difficulties was described by his C.O. as admirable.

Ordered in the evening to detail twelve men for wheeled-stretcher work, he went to the shed where his command waited. Holding a hurricane lamp high, he shouted: 'Noo then, you Fritzes. A dizzen o' ye! Compree?'

'Nein!' said a puzzled voice from among the Germans.

'*Nine*, ye gommeral? It's a nae nine, it's twal' o' ye! C'wa' noo! Look slippy! *You*, Nosey!' He pointed at a German with a long beak. 'And *you*, Breeks!' This time he jerked his thumb at a fellow whose trousers, at the rear, had lost an argument with some barbed wire.

Charlie fitted Nosey between the front handles of the stretcher and Breeks at the tail—a nice touch!—and then shoved them out of the hut. Rapidly he selected five other pairs of bearers and handed the lot over to an orderly.

'Noo, laddie, there's your Fritzes', he said. 'See ye dinna lose ony o' them. I canna afford to lose ony—the supply is streectly limited!'

Jock was always a man of few words and no deathless eve-of-battle speeches have come down to us. But other, briefer addresses have been recorded. One regiment—said to be the Highland Light Infantry—bought a silver cup for presentation to the retiring colonel, a popular officer. The officers and men of the regiment being assembled, the best spokesman among the officers picked up the cup and held it out at arm's length to-wards the colonel.

'Sir,' he said, 'there's the jug.'

The colonel said: 'Eh, is that the jug? All right. Thanks.'

And the whole embarrassing incident came to an end.

Highlanders have also been embarrassed by the regrettable fact that on occasions not all the men in Scottish units are Scottish by birth. There was a distinguished Scottish officer who never lost an opportunity to advertise his countrymen. One evening at mess he had a large number of guests. On duty behind his chair was a magnificent Highland piper and to draw attention to the man, the officer turned to him and said: 'What part of Scotland do you come from, my man?'

'Tipperary, your honour,' the piper replied.

About 1900 a Jewish officer was gazetted to a Highland regiment, much to the indignation of the senior major, who remarked to his brother officers in great wrath: 'Weel, weel, I've seen mony strange things in my time. We've had Hielanders frae England, we've had Hielanders frae Wales and we've even had them from Ireland, but in the whole course of my existence, gentlemen, this is the very first time we've had Hielanders frae Jerusalem!'

V

The Kilt

THE SCOTS have had many insults flung at their kilt. There have also been some compliments. The best was a German one, which has more value than one from an ally. During the Great War the Germans called the Scots 'those ladies from hell'. It was a good description, an apt likeness. No witches from the sulphuric depths ever fought with such fury as the kilted Scots. A part, perhaps a large part, of the Scot's fighting prowess resulted from the kilt, for Jock knew himself to be different from other soldiers and the kilt emphasized the simple fact. It gave him colour and glamour and it attracted women and war correspondents—and both spread his reputation far and wide.

A Highlander's dress has changed a great deal over the centuries, but it has always been distinctive and this, in itself, has served to give the Highland soldier his unique character.

Always the dress was practical. In the Middle Ages the men wore a woollen or linen garment, sometimes padded or quilted and often smeared with grease to make it waterproof. A deerskin and possibly a mantle was extra clothing.

Later, short woollen sleeveless jerkins were worn over knee-length linen shirts with wide sleeves. On top of this was the plaid, or mantle. The legs were always bare, while shoes were of raw leather. Some men wore a conical steel cap in battle, others had caps of otter or seal skin. Armour was never popular—perhaps partly because it was expensive—but 500 years ago some Highlanders wore a crude form of chain mail.

When the first Highlanders appeared in England, dressed in the kilt, they created quite a panic. The authorities did not approve of the garb, and attempts were made to persuade the new regiments to don the usual uniform. But Jock, who had never in his life worn anything but the kilt, refused now to part with it, and on that point he conquered.

The origin of the kilt has never been satisfactorily settled. Pictures are in existence showing that it was a part of the Highland dress in 1672, but there is no doubt that the Romans wore a similar attire when they invaded England.

It has been stated that the earliest dress of the Highlander consisted of 'a large woollen wrapper, extending from the shoulder to about the knee in one piece. Finding this garment inconvenient, some of the wearers, about 1728, separated the lower part from the upper, so that they might, when heated, throw off the upper and leave the lower, which thus became the philabeg, or short skirt.' Most Scotsmen, however, will not accept this explanation, as they maintain that the origin of the garb is 'lost in the mists of antiquity'.

They say that long before history began to be written in Scotland the kilt was the native garb of the Scottish High-lander. Sculptures of early date in rock and stone have been found in the Highlands and the Western Isles depicting Scots in the kilt. One of these later sculptures, said to be of the seventh century, displays the hanging purse or sporran that dangles in front of the kilt.

The earliest written record of the kilt, dated 1093, refers to short tunics and upper garments, which some authorities assume to refer to a plaid. A historian in 1512 described the Scots rushing into battle dressed in kilts daubed with paint and pitch. It was probably about this period that tartan patterns began to be produced. The kilt is described by a French writer in 1556 as a stained skirt of wool of various colours worn by the Highlanders (or wild Scots). A painting of the same period shows a jaunty band of kilted Scots on the march wearing hanging plaids and headed by a piper playing the bagpipes.

The British government was well aware that the kilt was, in effect, a dangerous weapon. After the Jacobite rising of 1745, the government passed the Act for the Abolition and Pros-cription of the Highland Dress, which read, in part: 'From and after the 1st day of August 1747 no man or boy within that part of Great Britain called Scotland, other than such as shall be employed as Officers and Soldiers in His Majesty's Forces, shall . . . wear or put on clothes commonly called Highland Clothes, that is to say, the Plaid, Philabeg or Little Kilt, Trowse, Shoulder Belts, or any part whatsoever of what peculiarly belongs to the Highlands.'

This Act was repealed in 1782, but before that, in 1757, the War Office made the first of its many attempts to abolish the kilt for the Highland regiments. It was forbidden to the 78th when they landed in North America in 1757 on the grounds that it was unfit for the severe winters and hot summers.

The officers and men protested and the C.O., Colonel Fraser, explained to the commander-in-chief that the men had a strong attachment to their national dress; he hinted, broadly, at 'the consequence that might be expected to follow' if they were deprived of it.

The order was countermanded and during the next six winters records show that the Scots were healthier than the men of regiments which wore breeches and the traditional 'warm clothing'.

Still, the Scots had to crack hardy on occasions. In Quebec in the winter of 1759 the Scots suffered more from cold than other regiments; sentries were relieved every hour to save them from frostbite. In the end, the nuns of the city knitted the Highlanders long woollen hose; Sir John Fortesque notes that the nuns did this 'perhaps as much for decency's sake as for charity's sake'.

In the campaign in Holland and Westphalia in 1794–5 the cold was so intense that brandy froze in bottles, but the Highlanders—men of the 78th, 79th and the 42nd—weathered the winter well. One writer records that although the troops suffered greatly from want of food the 78th were saved much sickness from the fact that they always wore the kilt, 'the warmth of which around the body is a wonderful protection against chills that lead to dysentery and the like'.

But such arguments in favour of the kilt did not impress the War Office: Scots were sent out to India in trousers!

Probably the most vehement, impassioned defence of the kilt was made in 1804 by Colonel Cameron of the Cameron Highlanders when asked for his views on the proposal to abolish the kilt.

The colonel wrote:

The Highlander has an exclusive advantage, when halted, of drenching his kilt in the next brook, as well as washing his limbs, and drying both, as it were, by constant fanning, without injury to either, but on the contrary feeling clean and comfortable; while the buffoon in tartan pantaloon, with all its hinged frippery (as some mongrel Highlanders would have it), sticking wet and dirty to their skin, is not easily pulled off and less so to get on again in cases of alarm or any other hurry, and all this time absorbing both wet and dirt, followed up by rheumatism and fevers which ultimately make great havoc in hot and cold climates. . . .

Pausing only to take breath Colonel Cameron went on:

The proposed alteration must have proceeded from a whimsical idea more than the real comfort of the Highland soldier, and a wish to lay aside the national garb, the very sight of which has upon occasions struck the enemy with terror and confusion. . . . I sincerely hope that his Royal Highness will never acquiesce in so painful and degrading an idea as to strip us of our native garb and stuff us into a harlequin tartan pantaloon.

Despite this caustic comment—and others like it—in 1809 George III ordered that new Highland regiments would not wear Highland garb. Officially, the reason given was that after heavy losses sustained by Highland regiments after the Battle of Corunna it was becoming difficult to find recruits to keep the regiments up to strength. Many possible volunteers did not like the kilt, the government said. The Scots themselves said that it was because 'the people of South Britain found the Scottish national costume objectionable'.

Highland garb was not officially countenanced even for regular regiments but some Highland regiments continued to wear it. The kilt was on the field at Waterloo and later was seen in the streets of occupied Paris. Scottish officers were frequently plagued by Parisian ladies who asked them what, if anything, they wore beneath the kilt. It is quite likely that on occasions they found out.

In 1823, after constant agitation, the royal decree was rescinded and most regiments were allowed to wear a form of Highland dress, though they were disgusted at now being forced to wear trews; some wore the pantaloons which so infuriated Colonel Cameron.

During the Crimean War the Russians were much struck

with the Highlanders. In the famous charge of the Heavy Brigade at Balaklava a Russian officer was among those taken prisoner by the Scots Greys. On being brought to the rear, he passed the 93rd Highlanders drawn up for battle, and, attracted by their appearance, he asked: 'What sort of soldiers are those in the petticoats?'

A waggish British officer replied: 'Oh, they are the wives of the men on the grey horses!'—meaning the Scots Greys.

In 1897, during the disturbances in Crete, the Seaforth Highlanders were landed to preserve order, and their appearance created the greatest sensation the island had experienced for many years. The Cretans themselves wore a kind of kilt, but they had never heard of British soldiers dressed in such attire.

A crowd of natives were gathered watching the Seaforths in camp, when a Highlander, for a bit of fun, shouted to them: 'Gae hame, ye dirty blackguards, an' scrub yersel's.'

One of the natives replied: 'Go home yourself, Scottish dog, and cover yourself up!' It turned out that the man had spent some years in England, and had learned the language.

Both the Boers and the natives in South Africa had some funny ideas about the Highlanders. The Boers had the fixed idea, before the war began in 1899, that the Gordons were compelled to wear kilts because of their defeat at Majuba Hill in 1881. Queen Victoria, so the Boers believed, refused to supply them with trousers until they had redeemed their character!

The Boers considered that the bravery of the Gordons at Elandslaagte, in 1899, was the result of a desire to wipe away the stain and earn the right to wear trousers like an ordinary soldier!

General Koch, a Boer commandant who was captured at Elandslaagte, said that the Boers had suffered most from 'the soldiers in little clothes, half-men, half-women'. The gallant Gordons had not forgotten that, after Majuba Hill, they were known as 'the Kaffirs clothed in kilts', and they were burning to avenge the insult.

At the beginning of the Boer War the Highland regiments had more men shot·than the other regiments, and it became evident at last that the kilts were being used by the enemy's marksmen as targets. This was the experience of the Gordons at Elandslaagte, as is shown by the following extract from a letter written by one of the wounded: 'In advancing from cover I got hit in the sporran top by a spent bullet, which struck sufficiently hard to knock me over. I scrambled up again, and went on a short distance, when another one went through my sporran lower down, through my pocket-book in same, and then between my legs without touching me. Immediately afterwards I was hit in the leg just above the hose.'

As a result of the large number of deaths which were obviously due to the conspicuous nature of the dress, orders were given for the sporran to be discarded during the remainder of the campaign, while a khaki apron was provided for the men to wear over the kilt. This covering up of the tartan afterwards proved of great advantage, as fewer men were seriously wounded.

The Highlander has had to suffer a lot of inconvenience for his liking for the kilt. In the Sudan War of 1898, for instance, the thorns of the zariba, or hedge, by which the Dervishes protected their camp, tore the bare legs of the Camerons as they were charging through. In fact, after a fight many of the Scots sat down to pull out the thorns.

In the Boer War, many men of the Highland Brigade were crippled in a peculiar way. When they were lying down in the firing line the men found that the heat of the sun was so intense that it blistered the skin and contracted the muscles at the back of the legs. On another occasion a famous Highland regiment was on the march, when some of the men accidentally disturbed several hives of bees. That regiment had never yet been put to flight by an enemy, but this time officers and men broke up, demoralized.

English soldiers have their own ideas as to the reasons why a Scotsman is so greatly attached to his kilt. Once, a number of Gordons and Lancashire Fusiliers were talking together, when the subject of the kilt turned up. Naturally the Highlanders bragged about the garment they wore, and said that only a Scotsman was hardy enough to be able to wear one.

One of the Lancashire men replied that Jock was talking rubbish. The Scots, he claimed, were forced to have the kilt because they could not wear trousers.

'How dae ye mak' that oot?' asked a surprised Gordon.

'You Highlanders have such big feet that you couldn't get them into a pair of trousers, so you have to wear the kilt!' the Fusilier said. And this, as usual, led to a fight.

The loyalty of the Scottish soldier to his kilt was proverbial. He never would admit that he could be cold wearing it. In fact, Highlanders suffering from cold in civilization's ordinary dress have been known to change into the kilt to get warm. There is a story, perhaps apocryphal, that a stranger, seeing a kilted Highlander shivering in a biting wind, asked: 'Sandy, are you cold with the kilt?'

'Na, na, mon,' he said, 'but I'm nigh kilt wi' the cauld!'

In a hot climate the kilt has obvious advantages. Once, in India, a native prince inspected the 93rd Highlanders (Argylls) and he was so greatly impressed with their splendid physique and magnificent bearing—and probably by their kilts—that he expressed a wish to buy the regiment. When he was told that it was not for sale, the wealthy prince was very annoyed. It was the first time he had come across a thing that he could not purchase.

Some people resented Jock's popularity. After Dargai a private of the Derbyshire Regiment wrote: 'The pipes struck up at Dargai and the instant the Gordons made a move the whole lot went together, and you couldn't tell one regiment from another. We were all mixed up. They will praise the kilt regiment. It's no use an English regiment trying to get on when there is a regiment with the kilts. The kilts put all the other regiments in the dark, no matter how successful the others might be.'

Well, perhaps the Scots have at times stolen the thunder of other regiments, but one hard fact is proved by records; that with few exceptions, wherever there was tough work and bloody work to do there was a Scottish regiment; the comparatively few Scottish regiments have seen as much action as the rest of the regiments of the British Army put together.

The historian of the Black Watch praised the kilt in use during the Great War. 'In the winter of 1914 the kilt proved itself as fully as it had done in the past. Officers and men can wade knee deep through the trenches and arrive in comparative dryness and comfort, unhampered by wet trousers or

clinging breeches. It undoubtedly prevented much sickness.
. . . The kilt apron served one purpose in keeping the kilt
clean in the trenches.'

Still, the kilt was not an all-purpose garment. General Sir
Ian Hamilton, serving in India with the Gordon Highlanders,
found it unsuitable for riding a horse on church parade; all
officers were required to be mounted for church parades.

'We did not wear drawers except at athletics or dancing on
a platform,' the general wrote, 'so you were apt to get the
skin of your thighs pinched between the stirrup leathers and
the saddle and it was not very comfortable—I mean, bareback
riding is all very well when applied to the pony but not to one's
own backside.'

The War Office war on the kilt broke out again in 1939
when it banned the garment because of its 'unsuitability for
mechanized warfare'. It could be worn only for ceremonial
occasions and for walking out.

In December that year the War Office issued to the 1st
Argylls trial under-garments to protect the wearer from the
effects of war gases. The colour of this under-garment was
pink! Worse, it looked remarkably feminine in its design.
Several pairs of this monstrosity were sent to the Argylls 'for
trial and report'. The Argylls' report was brief and to the
point and there was no further issue. The intriguing aspect of
the matter is—what sort of intellect dreamed up pink bloomers
for Scotsmen?

Still, Highlanders who took part in the raid on St. Nazaire
in 1942 were given special permission to wear the kilt—and
all the more aggressive they must have been for it.

The Argyll and Sutherland Highlanders took their kilts to
Korea. They did not wear them in action, but did so on every
opportunity out of the line.

No garment is issued for the purpose of wearing under the
kilt. Until fairly recently the only time a Scot wore anything
under the kilt was for Highland dancing and tug-o'-war.
Some men do now also wear shorts, but this is optional.

A few years ago a woman photographer visited the 1st
Battalion Seaforth Highlanders to take a picture of a piper for
a national Sunday newspaper. She told the pipe-major that
she would prefer a shot of a piper dancing, so swords were

obtained and the dance started. The lady could not get the shot she wanted. Eventually, she lay on the ground to get what she called a 'worm's eye view'. This shot, she mentioned to the pipe-major, would be 'different'. Well, she took her picture—but it never did appear in the paper. The Seaforths were not really surprised—but the lady may have been.

The last word on the kilt has not yet been written, but French General Joffre came close to saying it during the Great War: *Pour l'amour, oui, mais pour le guerre, non* (For love, yes, for war, no).

VI

The Pipes and Cold Steel

LIKE THE kilt, there is something about the pipes that puts extra spirit in a Scot's heart and makes him want to fight. No musical instrument has ever been so closely connected with war, or so significant in winning victory. A drum might beat troops doggedly into action, but only the pipes fill him with the fire and the fury.

Generals and colonels have known this, the pipers know it, the men know it. When, for some reason, a Scottish regiment has been deprived of its pipes in battle it has fought with less zest.

At the Battle of the Heights of Abraham (Quebec) in 1759, the general complained to a field-officer about the conduct of a Highland regiment which had been repulsed and driven back in disorder. He wanted to know how the reverse had occurred. 'Sir,' the officer said, 'you did wrong in forbidding the pipers to play this morning. Nothing encourages the Highlanders so much in action; even now it is not too late.'

'Then let them blow as they like', the general said, 'and send them in again.' The pipers played and the Highlanders charged—and this time they took their objectives.

When the 73rd Regiment was in India in 1778 General Sir Eyre Coote thought that the pipes were 'useless relics of barbarous ages and not in any manner calculated to discipline troops'. But the pipers made him eat his words.

At Porto Novo in 1781 the 73rd was the only European regiment among the army of 9,000 men, with whom Coote defeated Hyder Ali's force of 80,000. The 73rd led all the main attacks and, as Coote himself said later, the pipers always seemed to blow their hardest when the fire of the enemy was hottest. This so pleased Coote that he shouted, 'Well done, pipers! You shall have a set of silver pipes for this!' Later, he paid for the pipes, which were inscribed with his opinion of the pipers.

The pipes have had startling effect on the enemy, too. For instance, at Pondicherry in 1793, when the 72nd (Seaforths) were under heavy fire from the French and were suffering badly from the blazing sun, their C.O. ordered the pipers to play some pibroch music. The sound of the pipes was so incongruous and unfamiliar in that setting that almost at once the French fire slackened and after a time it stopped altogether as the French soldiers packed the walls of their fortress to listen to the sound.

At the Battle of Assaye, 1803, the musicians were ordered to attend to the wounded and carry them to the surgeons in the rear. One of the pipers, believing himself included in this order, laid aside his instrument and assisted the wounded.

For this he was afterwards reproached by his comrades. Flutes and hautboys, they thought, could be well spared; but for the piper, who should always be in the heat of the battle, to go to the rear with the whistles was a thing altogether unheard of. The piper soon had an opportunity of playing off this stigma; in the advance at Argaum he played up with such spirit that the men could hardly be restrained from rushing to the charge too soon and breaking the line. Colonel Adams had to tell him to silence his pipes because he was making the men too excited.

At the Battle of Vimiera, in 1808, George Clarke, a piper of the 71st, was wounded in both legs as his corps was charging up rising ground against the French. The Highlander propped himself up against a bank and continued to play his comrades on.

As the first company passed him he shouted: 'Gang along, my braw laddies; I canna be wi' ye fechtin' ony langer, but deil hae me if ye shall want music!'

The Highlanders were facing great odds and Clarke's act is said to have turned the day in their favour; they cheered Clarke as they drove the French back. He was still playing when his regiment came back from the fight. The Highland

Society presented him with a set of pipes elaborately orna-
mented and inscribed: *To George Clarke, piper of the 71st, as a
mark of the Society's approbation of his spirited and laudable
conduct at the Battle of Vimiera, in continuing to play upon his
pipes to animate the men after being himself severely wounded.*
Clarke later became official piper to the society.

At Waterloo the 79th Regiment (Cameron Highlanders)
formed part of Picton's division which was posted at the centre
of the British line. The division had already been engaged at
Quatre-Bras and had suffered casualties. It stood up to two
hours fire by French artillery, then was attacked by French
infantry; at this moment it mustered 3,000 men to the
French 13,000.

When the French paused to readjust their line Picton
ordered his division to fire a volley and charge. Immediately
the French were driven into confusion and although the 79th
were caught by enfilade fire while crossing a hedge they pressed
home their attack. A contemporary writer said: 'A good
regiment like the 79th may be destroyed—it cannot be
defeated. The men soon regained touch, and then woe to the
French soldiers. . . .'

Napoleon sent forward his cavalry to support his retreating
infantry; the British formed square.

At this moment of crisis and climax Piper Kenneth McKay
calmly stepped outside the square and, despite the attacking
French cavalry, marched around the square playing 'Cogadh
No Sith' (Peace or War). It was a magnificent gesture, an
imperious act—and the Highlanders loved it and fought all the
better for it.

During the battle which preceded the taking of Cawnpore
in 1857 a wounded piper used his pipes effectively to protect
himself. A rebel cavalryman rode down on him, sabre drawn,
ready to kill. The Scot went through the actions of loading
his big drone, then he brought it up to his shoulder as if about
to fire. The rebel swerved, swivelled around and rode off at
speed.

Pipers made themselves immortal at Dargai during the
North-West Frontier campaigns of 1897–8. At Dargai the
final attempt to carry the enemy position was made at 2.30
p.m. It was preceded by an incident reminiscent of the old

days when the commanding officer, removing his hat, harangued his men before going in.

After a message had been heliographed for a concentrated fire of guns on the peak, Lieutenant-Colonel Mathias turned to the regiment and said, 'Gordon Highlanders, the General has ordered that position to be taken at all costs—the Gordons will take it!'

Then Major Macbean sprang out of cover at the head of his company, and with a yell the Gordons swarmed from the protecting ridge into the zone of fire. Led by Colonel Mathias, with Macbean on his right and Lieutenant A. F. Gordon on his left—with the pipes skirling the 'Cock of the North'—the irresistible mass of waving kilts and white helmets swept on for the first rush.

A murderous hail tore up the dust in the hollow; Macbean went down, but cheered his men on as they passed by him. Piper Findlater fell, shot through both feet, but, struggling into a sitting posture, continued to play. The first rush was followed by a second, officers leading, and then by a third, and in forty minutes they had done the business with a roll of three officers and thirty men either killed or wounded.

As the leading companies breasted the steep zig-zag path, the troops on the other side of the basin followed in support, and the enemy, terrified at all this valour, scuttled down the opposite slopes of the hill, leaving little work for the British bayonet.

It was at first reported that Piper Milne had been the hero of Dargai—Milne was shot through the bagpipes in the Chitral campaign—but the official gazette settled the matter by awarding the V.C. to Piper Findlater and for several months he was probably one of the most talked-of men in the British Isles.

At Netley Hospital, the Queen, rather than allow her wounded soldier to stand, rose in her wheeled chair to pin the cross on his breast—and Findlater's triumph was complete.

Piper William Middleton, who spent twenty-one years in the Gordons, had his big moment at Kandahar. He was playing on his company when suddenly his pipes were hit by a bullet; they wheezed and stopped. Middleton sat down to mend them and the silence convinced his company that he was dead. But soon he was in action again.

After the action it was found that seven bullets had hit his accoutrements. Respectively, the bullets had gone through his pipes, knocked the brass off his helmet, gone through his kilt, knocked a button off his coat, torn a hole in his water-bottle, ripped his haversack and struck his heel. Middleton himself was untouched.

In the grim hopelessness of Magersfontein, Piper McKay of the 93rd played to rally his comrades in their defeat. A Black Watch man who heard the music said, 'We were past caring before we heard the pipes; the music put a bit of heart into us again.'

During the infantry charge at Elandslaagte and while the Gordons were advancing in fine style under heavy fire, a false recall was sounded by the canny Boers and the Highlanders faltered.

Captain Mullins, of the Imperial Light Horse, who was charging with the Gordons, yelled at the Gordons' officers, 'Don't let's have another Majuba!' A boy bugler of the Gordons showed that he had the same spirit as the pipers. He rushed forward and blew the 'Charge'. The Gordons rallied and the Boers were driven from their positions.

Some people, oddly enough, profess to dislike the pipes and their music, which one English general described as 'a horrible, tuneless screeching, an abomination of sound'. But that 'tuneless screeching', like the men it inspired, helped to win battles.

Just how effective the pipes could be, even in the tumult of modern warfare, was shown by Piper Daniel Laidlaw of the King's Own Scottish Borderers on 25 September 1915, when his regiment was about to go over the top for an attack on German trenches near Loos.

The Scots were being heavily shelled and were badly shaken from the effects of gas. Piper Laidlaw, noticing this, climbed on to the parapet and with superb contempt of danger marched up and down in the open, playing his company out of their trench and on to the attack with 'Blue Bonnets over the Border'.

His action won him the V.C. 'The effect of his splendid example was immediate and the company dashed out to the assault,' the official citation read. Piper Laidlaw continued to play his pipes until he was wounded.

Another thing that helped to win battles was cold steel—the Scots' favourite weapon, though perhaps the Highlanders delighted to use it more than the Lowlanders did. From boyhood all Highlanders were trained to use cold steel and it remained their favourite weapon. Up till about 1645 the Highlander used the *claidheamh mor* or 'big sword'—a two-handed weapon with a broad, double-edged blade from four to six feet long.

After 1645 this was replaced by the shorter and more readily handled broadsword. In the '15 and '45 Rebellions the basket-hilted broadsword was popular. A beautiful single-handed weapon, the blade was double-edged and grooved and in most cases, straight. It was used as a cutting weapon and the Highlander, a master of the 'drawing cut', could inflict frightful wounds with it.

Another favourite weapon was the dirk, which could be concealed among the folds of the plaid. A stabbing knife about eighteen inches long, it was normally worn in a sheath on the right side, but sufficiently towards the front so that it could be drawn with the left hand. The metal fittings were usually of brass and the carved handle was carefully shaped to give a firm grip for an upward thrust. Often a broken sword blade would be reshaped as a dirk, but many dirks were specially made. Some dirks are beautiful things, engraved as they often are with regimental battle honours. Two small sheaths on the main one held a small knife and fork, usually with cairngorm hilts. The *sgian dubh* or skean dhu was carried in the stocking, though for hundreds of years it was concealed from view, often under the armpit. It was both a tool and a weapon.

The Highlander carried bullets in his sporran and gunpowder in a horn slung over his shoulder. Individually he may have had other pieces of equipment, but traditionally a soldier travelled light, with his plaid as his blanket.

The Lochaber axe, now a rarity, had a cutting edge of about eighteen inches and it was secured, from a hook at the back, to a long, strong staff. It was wielded effectively against cavalry, but was too heavy and clumsy for close-quarter fighting—and this type of combat was what the Scot liked best of all.

In the early days before they became part of the British

Army, the Highlanders had a distinctive style of fighting, well described in the *Book of Scottish Anecdote*:

They advanced with rapidity, discharged their pieces when within musket length of the enemy, then throwing them down, drew their swords, and holding a dirk in their left hand with their target, they darted with fury on the enemy, through the smoke of their own fire. When within reach of the enemy's bayonets, bending their left knee, they, by their attitude, covered their bodies with their targets, and received the thrust of the bayonets, which they contrived to parry, while at the same time they raised their sword-arm, and struck at their adversaries. Having got once within their bayonets, and into the ranks of the enemy, the soldiers had no longer any means of defending themselves, the fate of the battle was decided in an instant, and the carnage followed; the Highlanders bringing down two men at a time, one with a dirk in the left hand, and another with a sword.

As soldiers of the British Army the Highlanders transferred their affection from the sword and dirk to the bayonet. In Egypt in 1801 a Highland regiment faced a French battery, strongly posted on high ground, with a regiment in front to guard it. The major gave the order, 'Fix bayonets!' then the command, 'Prime and load!'

At this point a voice came from the ranks. 'No prime and load, but charge baignets at once!'

The impatient Scot was Donald Black, formerly an Isle of Skye smuggler. He led the men in a wild charge that drove the French from their positions, leaving the Highlanders in control.

If the story is true—and it probably is—then Private Black may well have been in hot water for disobeying an order and inciting others to do likewise. But the incident does show the Highlanders' love of the bayonet and of a bonny fight.

Not that the Scots have always won their battles. The Highland Brigade of the Boer War lost one major fight—and the disaster shocked them. The brigade consisted at first of the 71st Highland Light Infantry, 73rd Black Watch, 78th Seaforths, and 91st Argylls, and was under the command of Major-General Andy Wauchope. It was these four regiments that met with the terrible disaster at Magersfontein. They were marching in close formation to attack the Boers in the dark when with dramatic and completely unexpected suddenness they were fired on, heavily and at close range. They had blundered headlong into Boer trenches, covered by wire and placed far ahead of where the Boers were expected to be and unknown to the British command. The fire was probably the heaviest and most sustained that British troops had faced at that time. Twenty-three officers and 148 men were killed and forty-five officers and 647 men wounded.

Among the killed were Wauchope himself and the colonels of the Black Watch and the Argyll and Sutherland Highlanders. The general fell while in the act of calling his men to rally round him; but no soldiers in the world could have stood that blaze of fire from the hidden Boers at only a few yards distance, and many of the men yet unharmed retreated. Some rushed heroically at the trenches, and one officer was just waving his hat and shouting, 'Now, boys, here we are!' when he fell dead with three bullets through his heart.

Despite their great loss and shock, there is good ground for believing that the Highlanders would have carried the trenches with the bayonet if the Boers had not raised a cry of 'Retire!' The men mistook this for an order given by their officers, and many fell back at the critical point of the charge.

The remnants of the brigade withdrew three hundred yards, and, taking cover, began to fire at any of the enemy who showed themselves. All the morning they sniped at the Boers—assisted by the Gordons, who had come up—and then, after lying for many hours in a broiling sun, they finally retired.

Many pathetic incidents occurred after the battle. A Scots Guardsman, who was with the escort to the artillery, said that when the Highlanders came back, some of them offered 10s. for a drink of water. Some of the wounded lay on the ground for thirty-one hours, without water or food, before the enemy would allow the ambulance to approach.

All these wounded, too, had to keep as still as possible while they lay, tortured by thirst, for the Boers shot at any man who moved. Lieutenant Graham, of the 1st Argylls wrote home to his father: 'There we lay in the broiling sun all day, and it took all the skin off my legs. I tried once to pull my hose up, but there was such a hail of bullets from the Boers, directly that a finger was moved, that I gave it up. While I was lying there with my rifle across my front—the thick butt in front of my head as a sort of protection—a bullet or shell came and carried away four inches off the top of my rifle.'

Soon after this the 1st Gordons were put into the Highland Brigade in place of the 71st Highland Light Infantry, and the whole force was then a kilted one. Men were rapidly sent from home to fill up the ranks of the regiments, and a new commander, in place of Wauchope—Major-General Hector Macdonald,* an old member of the Gordons and long known as 'Fighting Mac'.

The Highlanders had now what they considered a disgrace to wipe out, and before the end of ten weeks they did it at Paardeberg. Here the force that had fought them at Magersfontein was, by Roberts's decisive tactics, brought to bay, and Macdonald's men were among the first that drew round the enemy's position.

To reach their post in front of the enemy the brigade had made a remarkable march. After a hard day's tramp they had reached Klipkraal, where they were so tired they lay down and went to sleep in the ranks. Two hours later the tired regiments struggled to their feet and, half-asleep, continued the march.

The Highlanders went into battle, and by short rushes over open ground, where Boer bullets cut down many of them, they drew closer to the trenches of the Boers, who were now surrounded on every side. So deadly was the fire that on the open spaces men were pinned down for most of the day.

After a week's fighting the Gordons and the Canadians got so near the Boers that they hoisted the white flag. Over 4,000 of the enemy surrendered, and when their leader, Cronje, was received by Lord Roberts, a line was formed by a guard of the Seaforths. The Highlanders lost heavily in the battle; at the finish, in fact, only 1600 out of the 3200 who went to South Africa remained.

---

* He had joined as a private and worked his way up through the ranks.

VII

Scottish V.C. Winners

SCOTTISH REGIMENTS have won a total of 127 V.C.s*
since the award was instituted in 1854. They are made up this
way: Gordons 18; Seaforths 18; Argyll and Sutherland Highlanders 16; Black Watch 15; Cameronians and H.L.I. 13
each; Scots Guards 9 (including awards won when the regiment was known as the Scots Fusilier Guards); Royal Scots 7;
Royal Scots Fusiliers 6; King's Own Scottish Borderers 5;
Camerons 4; Scots Greys 2; Scottish Horse 1.

I have selected from the records one V.C. winner from each
regiment. The deeds for which the decoration was won are
varied, but each shows something of the Scottish character—
initiative, dash, independence and sheer doggedness.

*   *   *

THE ARGYLL AND SUTHERLAND HIGHLANDERS
*Major (temporary Lieutenant-Colonel) Lorne MacLaine Campbell,
D.S.O., T.D.*

On 6 April 1943, in Tunisia, Lieutenant-Colonel Campbell
was in command of a battalion of Argylls detailed to break
through a German minefield and anti-tank ditch and to form a
bridgehead for a brigade of the Highland Division.

In darkness and under heavy shell- and machine-gun fire
Campbell managed to lead his battalion into position, crossing

* The only formations to win more V.C.s than the Gordons and Seaforths are:
Royal Artillery (including Field, Garrison, Horse, etc.) 48; Royal Engineers 38;
Rifle Brigade 27; South Wales Borderers 22; King's Royal Rifle Corps 21; Royal
Fusiliers 19. The Lancashire Fusiliers and the R.A.M.C. have each won 18 awards.

an unswept minefield in the process and capturing 600 enemy. Reaching his objective, he found that a gap blown by the Engineers in the anti-tank ditch did not correspond with the vehicle lane already cleared in the minefield. Realizing the vital necessity of quickly establishing a gap for the anti-tank guns, he took charge of this operation. It was now broad daylight, but again under heavy fire he made a personal reconnaissance and established the vehicle gap.

After a hectic day, at four-thirty that afternoon heavy enemy attacks developed. It was now that Campbell's personality dominated the battlefield with a display of valour and utter disregard for personal safety which, to quote his citation, 'could not have been excelled'.

Always in the thick of the fight, he inspired his men to hang on. When one forward company was forced to give ground he went forward alone to them into a storm of fire and personally reorganized their position, remaining with the company until the attack was held.

Under close-range small-arms fire, he stood in the fight to direct the battle and was painfully wounded in the neck by shell-fire. He did not have the wound dressed until the tempo of the fight died down and even then he refused to be evacuated.

His citation says: 'There is no doubt that but for Lieutenant-Colonel Campbell's determination, splendid example of courage and disregard of pain the bridgehead would have been lost. This officer's gallantry and magnificent leadership when his now tired men were charging the enemy with the bayonet and fighting them at hand-grenade range, are worthy of the highest honour and can seldom have been surpassed in the long history of the Highland Brigade.'

It should be said, too, that in modern warfare it is difficult for a commanding officer to win a V.C. Lieutenant-Colonel Campbell's audacious action was reminiscent of the days of old, when a C.O. personally led his men from the front.

THE BLACK WATCH
Private Charles Melvin

During April 1917, at Istabulat, near Baghdad, Private Melvin's company had advanced to within fifty yards of the front-line trench of a redoubt but at this point, under intense fire, the company had to go to ground and wait for reinforcements.

Private Melvin, however, did not go to ground. He charged on alone, over ground swept by rifle and machine-gun fire. Reaching the enemy trench he stopped and fired two or three shots into it, killing one and possibly two of the enemy. When the other Turks in the trench continued to fire at him, Melvin became a little annoyed. He jumped into the trench and attacked the Turks with his bayonet, using it as a short sword; his rifle had been damaged and he could not 'fix' the bayonet.

Melvin's fierce and resolute attack panicked the enemy and most ran, but Melvin killed two and disarmed eight unwounded and one wounded. Melvin now took time off to bind the wounds of the injured man—an extraordinary enough act under the circumstances—then supporting the wounded man, he drove the eight unwounded men before him back to his own lines where he handed them over to an officer.

Melvin now obtained a load of ammunition and returned to the firing line, where he reported himself to the platoon sergeant. All this was done under intense small-arms fire and a heavy artillery barrage. Melvin's citation concludes with these words: 'Throughout the day Private Melvin greatly inspired those near him with confidence and courage.' Likewise, he must have filled the enemy with whom he came in contact with fear and dismay. It was no wonder the Germans called the Highlanders 'ladies from hell'.

THE QUEEN'S OWN CAMERON HIGHLANDERS
Sergeant Donald Farmer

During the attack on General Clements's camp at Nooitgedacht on 13 December 1900, Lieutenant Sandilands of the Camerons took fifteen men to the assistance of a picquet which was heavily engaged; most of the picquet were casualties.

A force of Boers, hidden by trees, waited until Sandilands's party was only twenty yards away—then they opened fire. Two men were killed and five wounded in the first volley.

Sergeant Farmer picked up the wounded and disabled officer and carried him to safety, under the heavy and close fire.

Then he returned to the firing line and was eventually taken prisoner. Perhaps Farmer's return to the action was more dramatic than his rescue of the officer. Nobody would have blamed him for staying out once he had got out; cold-bloodedly to charge back into the fight was the mark of great courage.

THE CAMERONIANS (SCOTTISH RIFLES)
Lieutenant William Rennie

Long before he won his V.C. during the Indian Mutiny Lieutenant Rennie had seen much service. He served with the 73rd in Montevideo during the blockade in 1846, during the Kaffir War of 1846–7 and that of 1850–3. He was present at many engagements, including the Battle of Berea and in 1854 was promoted ensign in the field for his gallant conduct.

He was promoted lieutenant into the 90th in February 1857 and with his previous record and the fighting then beginning in the Mutiny it might have been expected that Rennie would do something outstanding.

On 21 September 1857 Havelock's force was moving on Lucknow and the 90th had skirmishers out during the advance. The mutineers were putting down a heavy musketry fire to cover their guns, which were preparing to fire on the 90th. Lieutenant Rennie dug in his spurs and charged the guns, preventing the enemy from dragging off one gun, which was captured.

Charging guns is a hazardous business at any time, and a man is lucky if he gets away with it once, but Rennie tried it again four days later. The mutineers were firing grape—clouds of small shot—but Rennie charged straight for the guns and so fierce was he that the mutineers abandoned them.

The two incidents were outstanding for their gallantry, which was made even more commendable by the fact that Rennie's actions were cold-bloodedly thought out and were not merely hot-headed impulses.

THE GORDON HIGHLANDERS
Major George Stewart White

On 6 October 1879, at Charasiah, Afghanistan, the Gordons were ordered to take a fortified hill. When artillery and rifle fire did not dislodge the enemy, Major White led an attack on the hill, advancing with two companies of the regiment. The going was rugged and the men had to clamber from one steep ledge to another. Finally, exhausted, the Gordons came on a strongly positioned enemy force, outnumbering them by eight to one. Instant action was necessary and the Gordons were too exhausted to provide it. Major White took a rifle and going on alone shot the leader of the enemy. This act so intimidated the others that they ran—and the position was won.

Again, on 1 September 1880, at the Battle of Kandahar, Major White led a final charge against the enemy. The Afghans were supported by two guns and their rifle fire was heavy. White, mounted, rode straight for the guns and captured one of them. Once again, impressed by this daring act, the enemy withdrew from the position.

THE HIGHLAND LIGHT INFANTRY
Corporal David Fergusson Hunter

Corporal Hunter's citation in the *London Gazette* on 23 October 1918 reads, in part: 'For most conspicuous bravery, determination and devotion to duty. . . . Corporal Hunter's outstanding bravery, coupled with determination, fortitude and endurance is beyond all praise and is a magnificent example to all.'

When his battalion was sent to the front line in France to relieve another unit, Corporal Hunter was detailed to take over an advanced post in shell-holes close to the enemy. The relief was carried out in darkness and there was no opportunity to reconnoitre the adjacent ground.

The following afternoon the enemy drove back the posts on Corporal Hunter's flanks and established their own posts close to him and all around him. He was isolated, ringed by Germans.

Short of rations and water, Hunter told his few men that he would hold 'to the last'. He repelled several counter-attacks over the next forty-eight hours. Most of the time he had no food or water. On the evening of the second day he tried to make contact with his company, but without result.

Apart from the constant enemy attacks, Hunter had to endure the barrage fire of the enemy and of his own artillery. On the evening of the third day he was relieved by a regimental counter-attack. Seldom has a junior N.C.O. shown such qualities of leadership.

THE KING'S OWN SCOTTISH BORDERERS
Company Sergeant-Major John Skinner, D.C.M.

According to an historian of the Borderers, Company Sergeant-Major John Skinner was one of the most remarkable men of the British Army, apparently incapable of considering his personal safety or of understanding how anyone could enjoy a fight less than he did.

Skinner's bravery in the Great War was certainly outstanding. First of all he was awarded a D.C.M. for gallantry at Neuve Chapelle and in this and other actions he managed to accumulate eight wounds.

Then at Langemarck, in August 1917, came his crowning feat. His company was making an attack when a machine-gun opened on the left flank, delaying the advance. Skinner, though wounded in the head, took six men and with great courage and determination he worked around the left flank of three blockhouses from which the machine-gun fire was coming. He bombed and took the first blockhouse single-handed. Then he led his men to the other blockhouses, which he skilfully cleared, taking sixty prisoners, three machine-guns and two trench-mortars.

'The dash and gallantry displayed by this warrant-officer enabled the objectives to be reached and consolidated,' Skinner's V.C. citation reads.

A sniper killed Skinner on 17 March 1918. The esteem in which the Army held this man was shown by the great funeral accorded him; six V.C. winners acted as his pall-bearers.

Born in Glasgow, Skinner enlisted at the age of sixteen and had seen seventeen years' service before he died. He was wounded three times in the Boer War. His medals are now the most honoured relics in the regimental museum at Berwick-on-Tweed.

THE ROYAL SCOTS

Temporary Captain Henry Reynolds, M.C.

On 12 April 1917, at Zonnebeke in Flanders, Captain Reynolds's company was approaching its final objective when it suffered heavy casualties from enemy machine-guns and from an enemy pill-box, which had been passed by the first British wave.

Captain Reynolds organized his men, who had become scattered. Then, alone, he made for the pill-box, scrambling from shell-hole to shell-hole; all the time he was under very heavy machine-gun fire. Near the pill-box he threw a grenade, but the Germans had blocked the entrance and the grenade exploded harmlessly.

Reynolds then crawled right to the entrance and forced a phosphorous grenade inside, setting fire to the post. Three enemy died and the remaining eight surrendered with two machine-guns. Later, though wounded, Captain Reynolds continued to lead his company against another objective, which he captured with seventy prisoners and two more machine-guns. The entire operation was carried out under heavy machine-gun fire from the flanks, but Reynolds kept complete control of his men at all times.

THE ROYAL SCOTS FUSILIERS

Private David Ross Lauder

Lauder won his cross for one of the most remarkable acts in V.C. history. In 1915, at Gallipoli, he was a member of a bombing party retaking a sap captured by the Turks. He threw a bomb, but it failed to clear the parapet and fell among the Fusiliers' bombing party.

There was no time to smother the bomb or to pick it up and throw it again so Lauder did the only thing he could. He put his foot on it. The foot was blown off, but his mates were unhurt.

This act showed something of Scottish military character—the unwritten rule that comrades should not suffer for one man's mistake. The instantaneous courage needed to put a foot on a grenade is incredible.

THE SEAFORTH HIGHLANDERS
Sergeant Alexander Edwards

Near Ypres, on 31 July 1917, Sergeant Edwards located an enemy machine-gun in a wood and taking a small party he led a courageous attack on the gun; he killed the crew and captured the gun.

The same day a sniper was causing casualties among men of the sergeant's company, so he crawled out to stalk the sniper. He was badly wounded in the arm while stalking, but he went on and killed the sniper. Stalking a sniper is, if possible, more dangerous than rushing a machine-gun, but it was the type of task at which a Highlander excelled.

Only one officer was now left with the company. Sergeant Edwards, realizing that the success of the operation depended on the capture of the furthest objective, remained on duty, despite his wound, and led his men on until the objective was taken.

He wasn't through yet. He showed great skill in consolidating his position and 'very great daring' in personal reconnaissance. Next day Edwards, still on duty, was twice wounded, but as his citation records, 'he maintained a complete disregard for personal safety and his high example of coolness and determination engendered a fine fighting spirit in his men.'

THE SCOTS GUARDS
Sergeant John McAulay, D.C.M.

In an attack at Fontaine Notre Dame, on 27 November 1917,

when all the officers of his company were down, Sergeant McAulay assumed command and under shell- and machine-gun fire successfully held and consolidated the objective gained. He reorganized the company, cheered on and encouraged the men and under heavy fire at close quarters showed utter disregard of danger.

McAulay noticed that a counter-attack was developing on his exposed left flank. Being a Scot, he didn't wait for it to develop; he repulsed the attack by skilful and bold use of machine-guns. Aided by only two men, he caused heavy enemy casualties.

McAulay's company commander was mortally wounded and with typical Scottish concern for officers, he carried the O.C. a long distance to a place of safety. Twice he was knocked down by bursting shells but with dogged persistence he continued on his way. Once he had to put down his burden while he killed two Germans who tried to stop him.

The official citation concludes: 'Throughout the day this very gallant non-commissioned officer displayed the highest courage, tactical skill and coolness under exceptionally trying circumstances.'

THE ROYAL SCOTS GREYS
Sergeant Henry Ramage

Sergeant Ramage won his cross on 26 October 1854 at the Battle of Balaklava, but not content with one act of bravery, Sergeant Ramage performed three.

First of all, he saw Private MacPherson of his own regiment surrounded by seven Russians. Ramage galloped headlong to the scene, fought off the Russians and allowed MacPherson to escape. Two against seven was long odds, but a Scot with his dander up was worth several men.

A little later, when the Heavy Brigade was rallying after its amazing charge, and the enemy retiring, Ramage could not force his horse to move. Angry with the horse and determined to get into the fight, Ramage dismounted, fought on foot and brought in a Russian prisoner.

Finally, when the Heavy Brigade was covering the retreat

of the Light Cavalry, Ramage came across Private Gardiner, severely wounded by a round-shot but still astride his horse. Under very heavy crossfire Ramage got Gardiner on to his own horse and carried him to the rear. The sergeant had quite a busy day!

VIII

Life in the Army

BEFORE WE look at the remarkable lives of the Scottish regiments it is well to know something about the life in the Army of the men who made these regiments, for such qualities as heroism. endurance, dash and enterprise can only be properly seen and appreciated against the background of conditions at the time. And conditions were tough. Let's look at soldiering in the early nineteenth century, when the prestige of the British fighting man was high and climbing higher.

These were the days of close-quarter fighting, when men stood shoulder to shoulder to fight. The idea of crawling from cover to cover with the object of cutting an enemy's throat silently was considered unmanly and unsoldierly.

Armies, brigades, battalions and platoons were moved about the field like so many chess pieces and usually the commanding general had a place of vantage from where he could observe the movements of his enemy and then deploy his own troops accordingly.

Nearly always a battle depended on two things—in the beginning the coldly clever brain of the general and at the end the dogged determination of the private soldier. Almost inevitably any battle would devolve into a hand-to-hand fight between opposing infantry regiments or with an infantry regiment standing to an enemy cavalry charge.

Battles had to be fought at close quarters because muskets had an accurate range of less than a hundred yards; there was no point in firing at greater range. Many times infantry advanced to within twenty yards before firing. And as reloading took about a minute every shot had to count.

At the battle near Aboukir Bay, Egypt, in 1801, French and British, including the Black Watch, threw stones at each other when they ran out of bullets and then, of course, the fight came to the bayonet.

Today a soldier takes what shelter he can. In those days the men stood steady in their ranks perhaps for hours, while enemy cannon-balls tore through the ranks. This was a tough test of discipline, both imposed and personal. On the restricted front of battle, from a few hundred yards to, rarely, three or five miles, bodies would lie in heaps about the troops still standing.

Why didn't the men move? Why stand up and be slaughtered? There was a good reason. If infantry were caught out of formation the hovering cavalry would pounce and cut them to ribbons. The only real infantry defence against cavalry was steadiness in square. As men fell, so the survivors closed their ranks, always presenting that shoulder-to-shoulder wall of resistance.

Just how bloody battles could be can be seen by Waterloo. At the end of the day's fighting more than 45,000 dead and wounded, Allied and French, lay on the field, all within an area of a few square miles. Wellington, riding across the field that night, must have found it difficult to avoid the bodies of the dead and the groaning, sobbing wounded.

Mercer of the Royal Artillery was later to give one of the most graphic descriptions of the field. He wrote:

Of 200 fine horses with which we had entered the battle upwards of 140 lay dead, dying or severely wounded. Of the men scarcely two-thirds of those necessary for four guns remained and these so completely exhausted as to be totally incapable of further effort. Our guns and carriages were intermingled with dead and dying horses. . . . Here and there some poor wretch, sitting up amidst the countless dead, busied himself in endeavours to staunch the flowing stream with which his life was fast ebbing away. . . . From time to time a figure would half raise itself from the ground, and then, with a despairing groan, fall back again. Others, slowly and painfully rising would stagger away with uncertain steps across the field in search of succour. Many after staggering a few paces would sink again on the ground with their entrails hanging out. . . . Horses there were, too, in like state. One poor animal excited painful interest—he had lost I believe, both his hind-legs and there he sat the long night through on his tail. . . . Although I knew that killing him at once would be mercy I could not muster courage enough to give the order. Blood enough I had seen shed during the last thirty-six hours and sickened at the thought of shedding more.

Only five yards from where Mercer slept under one of his gun-carriages a badly wounded French grenadier lay groaning all night.

Of the scene the following morning Mercer gives another grim picture:

One of my sergeants came to ask if they might bury Driver Crammond 'because he looks frightful'. I walked to the spot and certainly a more hideous sight cannot be imagined. A cannon shot had carried away the whole head except barely the visage, which still remained attached to the torn and bloody neck. The men said they had been prevented sleeping by seeing his eyes fixed on them all night. . . .

Numerous groups of peasants were moving about busily employed stripping the dead and perhaps finishing those not quite so. Some of these men I met fairly staggered under the enormous load of clothes, firearms, swords, etc., and many had large bunches of crosses and decorations. . . .

Mercer describes how he came upon a whole regiment of British infantry asleep in columns. Not far from the sleeping men lay two Irish light-infantry men 'sending forth such howlings, wailings, oaths and execrations as were shocking to hear. One of them had his leg shot off, the other a thigh smashed by a cannon-ball.'

Mercer found a well and took some of his men on a tour of the many wounded men, giving each a drink of water. Many French wounded begged him to kill them at once, since they would rather die by the hand of a soldier than be left to the mercy of the Belgian peasants. And Mercer well knew that the Belgians would murder the French out of hand.

Mercer also visited Hougoumont, scene of some particularly frightful carnage; the field here was more thickly strewn with corpses than elsewhere and the ditches were full of them. Many soldiers had died in a barn which had been set on fire and amid the ruins Mercer saw men sitting up, trying to bandage their wounds.

The ghastly scenes after Waterloo were not exceptional. Waterloo differed from many other battles only in its magnitude. A wound in Spain or in India or in America hurt just as much as one at Waterloo.

A fight was sometimes less arduous than a long march, on which suffering could be extreme. Yet the infantry bore their hardships with, generally, uncomplaining stoicism. During the Peninsular campaigns one officer wrote: 'I have often seen the blood soaking through the gaiters and over the heels of the soldiers' hard shoes, whitened with the dust.'

Sweat-soaked, exhausted men would sometimes fall and lie, conscious but unable to summon another ounce of will. When a man was badly wounded he usually lay in the field until he died; if he could walk he dragged himself to the rear, hoping to find a doctor to help him. Wounded men sometimes tramped for hundreds of miles under dreadful conditions. Today a soldier classed as 'walking wounded' does not, as a rule, have much wrong with him; in Peninsular days many such a man was half dead.

The Scots were clannish and unwounded men helped along a suffering mate as best they could; it went very much against the grain of a Highlander to be forced to abandon a comrade to the enemy.

Often, a man's sufferings only began when he was carried or when he staggered into the barn or church being used as a hospital. Here surgeons in short sleeves wielded saw and knife and probe with more enthusiasm than skill, amid a foul mess of blood, rags and dirt.

Less than fifty per cent of wounded could expect to survive gangrene, loss of blood or tetanus. Operations were performed without anaesthetic, hence surgical shock was severe and often fatal. The wonder of it is that any wounded man survived. In the Crimea about 4,000 men were killed in action while more than 20,000 died of disease and wounds, often in hospital.

The Highlanders were tough, but still they suffered. A contemporary writer, describing the march on Madrid after the Battle of Salamanca, 1812, tells of the Highlanders' plight: 'The carts to the rear of the column were full of wounded, dying and exhausted Highlanders, speechless and groaning, the living as pale as the dead, all covered with dust from the battlefield. Their feather bonnets and torn tartan plaids hung on the pointed stakes which formed the sides of the cart.'

There is nothing so pathetic as a desecrated feather bonnet, looking bedraggled and unowned, all its pride vanished.

An officer, if he was lucky, might be billeted on a family kindly enough to care for him until he had recovered. Vinegar was the only antiseptic, disinfectant and dressing for wounds. Typhus, caused by lice, killed many soldiers who had survived wounds, while dysentery and ague (probably malaria) was common.

Illness was a terrible enemy. In the eight weeks of the imbecile Walcheren Island expedition in 1809—intended as part of an attack on Antwerp and the Schelde—7,000 men died, 14,000 had their health ruined permanently and many more thousands were ill, mostly from malaria.

Water was always a problem; it was not chlorinated and nearly always men drank it unboiled, sometimes with frightful results.

Besides their weapons, the marching infantry of the early nineteenth century carried their house on their back. In a man's knapsack were three pairs of shoes and an extra pair of soles and heels, spare socks and shirt, a greatcoat or blanket. Strapped to the knapsack was a tin camp-kettle—one between six men and carried in turn. In the haversack, worn at the hip, was a clasp-knife, fork, spoon, tin mug and other personal gear and three days' rations. The daily ration was 1 lb. of beef, 1 lb. of biscuit and a tot of rum or wine. The water bottle was filled and there was a hatchet, bayonet, musket and eighty rounds of ammunition. The total weight was appalling and, what was worse, it was awkwardly placed.

A hideous custom at this time was the regulation which demanded a pigtail and powdered hair for soldiers. Old barracks, like the gentry's houses, had their powdering rooms. Powdering was a painful process, as described by one soldier of the time. 'The hair required to be soaped, floured and frizzed, in order to be tortured into an uncouth shape, which gave the man acute pain and robbed him of the power of turning his head easily, unless he brought his body around with it.'

In some regiments the coiffure was worked up with the aid of rancid suet, whitening and meal. The pigtail, or queue, was tied up with a bow of ribbons. The custom continued until July 1808, but even then some queues were worn until 1812. The condition of a man's hair and scalp must have been dreadful after heavy rain.

Usually the men had no tents, no covering at all. During the Peninsular War, pre-Waterloo, they were often soaked in rain and many had no shoes. Rations were scarce and often arrived just as the order was given to continue the march. The food was merely a hacked-off lump of meat, still bloody from field butchery, together with hard biscuits. In a man's haversack the two often became worked into a mash, which must have been horrible to eat.

A favourite topic of debate among soldiers was which was the worst soldiering season—summer or winter. Was it better to fry or freeze? Actually, their opinions were adjustable according to what they were suffering at the time of discussion. During the retreat in the winter of 1812 in the high country of Spain any man would have volunteered for service in the Sahara.

Amenities were non-existent; there was not even a tobacco ration. A private soldier was not supposed to need amenities—although officers usually dined well in comfortable quarters. Some of them needed a dozen horses to carry their gear, which on occasions included dressing-tables and easy chairs.

With few exceptions officers cared very little for the welfare of their men—and these exceptions were generally to be found in the Highland regiments. Very few generals made it their business to see that their men were well fed, clothed and comfortably camped or billeted.

Young officers of the day knew nothing about their craft and before 1802 there was no Royal Military Academy to teach them. By practice—and by instinct if they were lucky—they picked up the tricks of the trade. But for all their ignorance the great majority were brave to the point of recklessness and under fire they knew how to set an example to the men. They gambled and drank, these young men, and they played the devil with women, but if they survived the battles they made good soldiers. Some of them had much more to their make-up than they liked to pretend. The officer the men liked best was the man who was tough, but just. They knew instinctively that he would bring them out of a fight if possible.

Home leave was practically non-existent. Many a soldier served overseas from shortly after his enlistment until his retirement; an unbroken spell of ten years abroad was commonplace. If a married man was lucky he could take his wife with him on service—but as only five or six wives per company were allowed he had to be very lucky indeed. What these women endured and suffered cannot be imagined.

Many soldiers did not particularly want to go home because they felt they were not wanted there. To the civilian Englishman there was nothing much lower than a 'common soldier'—especially in times of peace. This attitude persisted until Edwardian times.

Discipline was not merely severe—it was cruel, though much more so in English regiments than in Scottish ones.

As Wellington himself said, strict discipline was necessary in most English regiments, which always had a proportion of very doubtful characters indeed, some of them vicious and unprincipled. Not all of them had enlisted for love of king and country and not all wanted to fight.

The Highlander, however, nearly always enlisted not only willingly, but eagerly; to him soldiering was the most honourable profession possible. Beyond this he had great natural pride in his regiment. This pride came to the English soldiery, too, it must be said, but sometimes only after a long period.

Flogging in most regiments occurred almost daily; it was the punishment for such minor crimes as petty theft or brief absence without leave. Once during the Peninsular War General Crauford saw two soldiers leaving the ranks. He halted the brigade and ordered a drum-head court martial; the two men were sentenced to a hundred lashes—although the French, at this moment, were not far behind the retreating British column.

Close to the general a private soldier muttered: 'Damn his eyes! He had much better get us something to eat than badger us this way.' Crauford heard these words and had the man court martialled. Three hundred lashes. And, asking not to be tied up, he stood and took his punishment without a murmur. One of the spectators was his own wife, who treated his mutilated back when it was all over.

Occasionally the maximum sentence of 1200 lashes was given and, not to be wondered at, some men died under the lash. One soldier, Sergeant Mayberry, was given 700 lashes for embezzlement of company funds; then he was reduced to the ranks. Surprisingly, Mayberry did not become embittered; he volunteered for the first draft to leave for the Peninsula and fought with great heroism at the storming of Badajoz, where he was killed in action.

Even so mild a man as Sir Charles Napier, who was considerate of the men under his command, was an advocate of flogging. Here is what he wrote to his mother when he was commanding the 50th Regiment in 1808:

> You know my antipathy to flogging: you know that it is unconquerable. . . . Still, as other severe punishments do not exist in our army we must use torture in some cases, until a substitute is given by our government.
>
> Mark this narrative. A robbery was committed in the regiment and the thief was discovered in a few hours. . . . I resolved to make a severe example . . . he was sentenced to 900 lashes. Yet there was not one positive proof of robbery—all was presumptive evidence. . . . Yesterday he was flogged in the square. When he received 200 lashes he was promised pardon if he told where the money was. No! God in heaven was his witness that he was innocent. I was inexorable; and it is hardly credible that he received 600 lashes, given in the most severe manner. At six hundred lashes he was taken down, with the seemingly brutal intention of flogging him again on a half-healed back . . . the greatest torture possible. Pain, lowness and the people employed to frighten him succeeded; he confessed all, and told where the money was hid.

Writing in 1837, Napier said: 'I have seen many hundreds of men flogged, and have always observed that when the skin is thoroughly cut up and flayed off the great pain subsides. Men are frequently convulsed and screaming during the time they receive from one lash to 300, and then they bear the remainder, even to 800 or 1000 lashes, without a groan.'

Captain John Kinkaid of the Rifle Brigade, a compassionate and very humane soldier, wrote: 'Where soldiers are to be ruled there is more logic in nine tails of a cat than in the mouths of a hundred orators.' Kinkaid wrote much in defence of General Crauford and his cat.

Hanging, too, was common; Wellington and other generals of his time hanged men out of hand for looting.

Today a voyage on a troopship is rather a pleasant holiday. To the soldiers of 1800 a troopship was a floating hell. The men and their families were packed into decks too low for a man to stand upright, with no space, no furniture or fittings and no privacy. The food was appalling and as the trip went on it became worse; fruit and vegetables were only obtainable on the rare occasions when a ship put into a transit port. Such accepted modern amenities as baths, reading and recreation rooms were non-existent. When disease broke out—which, inevitably, was frequently—men died in hundreds. But strangely, these men and their no less gallant wives, took all their hardships in their stride, though many were discharged, literally worn out, at the age of thirty-five.

Not until 1881, the year of the climax of the great reforms organized by Edward Cardwell, Secretary of State for War, did conditions improve generally, with better barracks, better canteens, a finer appreciation of men's rights and such amenities as organized sport.

Whatever inspired men to join the Army in the early nineteenth century it certainly was not the pay. At the time of the Peninsular War an infantry private soldier was paid 1s. a day, but this was nominal pay only, for in barracks 5s. 6d. a week was stopped from this for messing, washing and 'sundries'. A cavalryman was paid 1s. 3d. a day, with a deduction of 7s. 1½d. a week. After Waterloo Wellington was paid £61,000 prize money, privates received £2 11s. 4d.

One general after another made a reputation leading to honours and riches, but very few gave credit to those to whom they owed their position—that incredible infantry. They could be dour or humorous, sentimental and pious or blasphemous and bitter; they were sometimes drunk, they could be ruthless one minute and gentle the next. And, on a few occasions they got out of hand in wild orgies of pillage and rape. But above all they were tried, seasoned and loyal soldiers. They were fighters.

When reading about the Scottish regiments, then, it is well to remember the background of the men in their ranks and the qualities they were expected to display—endurance, patience, stoicism, courage, loyalty.

It is important to remember, too, that while the Scots fought like devils—particularly the Highlanders—when a fight was over they seemed contrite and would go to great lengths to ease the sufferings of enemy wounded. Several observers have commented on this aspect of the Scottish soldier, emphasizing that he was not vindictive or cruel. And this is as it should be—in a man.

The Regiments

THE TWELVE regular regiments are dealt with in their order of Army seniority. Until 1881, when the far-reaching Cardwell reforms took place only the first twenty-five regiments of the British Army had two battalions. Consequently, it will be seen in the following histories that the second battalion of the Scots Guards, the Royal Scots Fusiliers, the Royal Scots and the King's Own Scottish Borderers have no separate chronological history.

In 1881 regiments were paired, with this effect on the Scottish formations: the 26th and 90th became the Cameronians (Scottish Rifles); the 42nd and 73rd the Black Watch; the 71st and 74th, the Highland Light Infantry; the 72nd and 78th the Seaforth Highlanders; the 75th and 92nd the Gordon Highlanders; the 91st and 93rd the Argyll and Sutherland Highlanders. The 79th—Queen's Own Cameron Highlanders —remained the only single-battalion regiment in the British Army until 1897 when a second battalion was raised.

In 1948 the first and second battalions of most regiments were combined and in more recent years other more sweeping amalgamations have taken place. Details are given in the year-by-year summaries of changes of titles which begin each chapter.

IX

The Royal Scots Greys

2ND DRAGOONS

1678–1707 The Royal Regiment of Scots Dragoons
1707–1751 The Royal Regiment of North British Dragoons
1751–1866 The 2nd or Royal North British Dragoons
1866–1877 The 2nd Royal North British Dragoons (Scots Greys)
1877–1920 The 2nd Dragoons (Royal Scots Greys)
1920– The Royal Scots Greys (2nd Dragoons)

Nicknames: the Greys; the Bubbly Jocks; the Bird Catchers

THE ONLY regular regiment of Scottish cavalry, and the oldest regiment of dragoons in the British Army, the Scots Greys were raised in Scotland in 1678, and in their earlier years were known successively as the Royal Regiment of Scots Dragoons, the Grey Dragoons, and the Scots Regiment of White Horses.

The distinctive head-dress of the Scots Greys was the grenadier bearskin. This was conferred upon them in honour of their routing and capturing the standard of the Regiment du Roi at the Battle of Ramillies, and was a style of head-dress worn by no other cavalry regiment in the British Army. Nor is there any other regiment of horse that has won greater glory on the field, or made its name such a symbol of all that is chivalrous and daring and gallant in the romance of war. It has lived magnificently up to the proud motto 'Second to None', which it has worn for 250 years.

Like every other regiment it has its nicknames, and is spoken of familiarly as 'the Bubbly Jocks' or as 'the Bird

Catchers'—the latter commemorating its capture of the Eagle of a French regiment at Waterloo.

Among the chief campaigns and battles of the Scots Greys are the following:

Flanders, 1694–7	Dettingen, 1743	Tournay, 1794
Germany, 1702–13	Fontenoy, 1745	Waterloo, 1815
Blenheim, 1704	Roucoux, 1746	Netherlands, 1815
Ramillies, 1706	Germany, 1758–63	Balaklava, 1854
Oudenarde, 1708	Minden, 1759	Inkermann, 1854
Malplaquet, 1709	Warburg, 1760	Tchernaya, 1855
Bouchain, 1711	Wilhelmstahl, 1762	Sebastopol, 1855
Flanders, 1742–8	Flanders, 1793–5	South Africa, 1899– 1902

At Blenheim they charged the retreating French and twelve squadrons of cavalry and twenty-four infantry battalions surrendered. None of the Greys was killed—though many were wounded—and it was at the head of the regiment that Marlborough placed himself when meeting visiting leaders. At Ramillies they charged through the village of Autréglise and forced the Regiment du Roi to surrender and yield up its colours and arms. The Greys captured sixteen or seventeen colours that day.

Nearly forty years later, in 1743, the Greys had another big moment at Dettingen. With James Campbell leading them— and well aware that they were invincible—they charged the French cuirassiers. It must have been a picturesque sight—the Dragoons with their high grenadier caps, red coats, blue waistcoats, and immense jack-boots, thundering towards the brilliant steel-encased Household Cavalry of France. The impact was terrific, the fighting sharp; then the French broke in confusion, leaving their magnificent white standard in the Greys' hands. Despite their reckless courage, the Greys did not lose a trooper. A field officer wrote: 'The Greys have escaped best, though they took most pains to be demolished.' It was a typical Scottish feat.

But at the Battle of Val (Laffeldt) in 1747 the Greys were badly mauled, although Sir John Ligonier led them with great dash against the enemy. They pierced and scattered two lines of cavalry and captured several standards, but their impetuosity carried them too far and they came under fire from concealed infantry.

After other campaigning, the Greys, at Waterloo, gave the world one of the most dramatic pictures of military history. Napoleon, after directing the attack against Hougoumont, massed his troops for a heavy attack against La Haye Sainte. Wellington ordered up fresh troops to the threatened point, among them the Scots Greys. Napoleon sent in d'Erlon's grenadiers who advanced with such resolve that the Belgians, in the Allied front line, broke and ran. The French then opened such a heavy fire on the British regiments that they began to give ground.

Pack's brigade—the Royal Scots, 42nd, 44th and 92nd regiments—were pushed in and their fire halted the French. At this moment the cavalry burst through a hedge which had concealed them and charged headlong at the French. As they rode through the intervals which the foot soldiers opened to allow their passage, the Highlanders caught hold of the stirrups of the Greys and charged with them.

The shout 'Scotland for ever!' was probably one of the most spontaneous and violent ever heard on a battlefield. In the first charge 2000 prisoners were taken. Sergeant Ewart of the Greys immortalized himself by capturing a French standard, after a fierce fight for it.

But Ewart was involved in another incident in the fight— and this one has rarely been told. A young cornet of the Greys, named Kinchant, asked Ewart to spare the life of a French officer whom he was on the point of cutting down. Ewart obeyed, though unwillingly, as he thought this hardly the time to be taking prisoners. Kinchant, to whom the officer surrendered his sword, ordered him in French to go to the rear. Ewart prepared to resume his work but hearing a shot looked round and saw that the Frenchman had shot Kinchant dead with a pistol. Ewart instantly wheeled round and the Frenchman pleaded for mercy. 'Ask mercy of God,' Ewart said, 'for the deil a bit will ye get at my hands!' And with one sweep of his sabre he took the man's head clean off.

The comments of the rival generals about the Greys became common knowledge at the time. Napoleon said: '*Ces terribles chevaux gris.*' Wellington: 'Would that there were more of the Greys!'

Unhappily, few of the Greys and few of the rest of the Union brigade survived the battle. Battle-mad, they galloped on and on, refusing to answer to the bugles' call of 'Rally'. Those who survived this first charge took part in others during the day, so that their numbers dwindled. At one time a dragoon, waiting on his horse for orders, was shot and killed by a French sniper and, weirdly, sat his horse until somebody removed him. At the end of the day, according to one report at the time, only thirty-three officers and men remained on duty.

At Schellenberg the regiment was dismounted and fought as infantry, helping to storm the trenches and drive the French and Bavarians across the Danube.

The Greys' performance at Balaklava was even more impressive than its deeds at Waterloo, but, regrettably, the charge of Scarlett's Heavy Brigade has always been overshadowed by that of the Light Brigade. This is a tragedy, because the Light Brigade's charge, after all, was a failure; that of the Heavy Brigade an astonishing, dramatic success.

Early on the morning of 25 October 1854, the Russian army made an attempt to force the position at Balaklava; as a preliminary step an attack was made on the chain of redoubts on Causeway Heights. The redoubts captured, large masses of Russian cavalry, supported by powerful artillery, poured over the ridge into South Valley. It was to check their advance that the Heavy Brigade—the Royals, Greys and Inniskillings (old comrades of Waterloo) and the 4th and 5th Dragoon Guards— was sent forward. The attack was commenced by the Greys and the Inniskillings.

The Russian cavalry was possibly 3,500 strong; the Greys and Inniskillings, under a fine old soldier, Brigadier Scarlett, numbered just 300. Kinglake says that the Greys 'gave no utterance other than a low, eager, fierce moan of rapture—the moan of outbursting desire.' A poetic description, but an apt one, of Scottish battle fervour.

Seeing the British cavalry, the Russian horse stopped. Scarlett's 300, gathering speed, charged hell for leather right at the mass of Russians, hitting them like some immense cannon-ball and with such force that many of the Greys cut their way right through the Russians and back again. In the midst of this the Royals and the 4th and 5th Dragoon Guards rode at the flanks of the Russians, giving a short breathing space to Scarlett's men.

High above the din a great voice shouted 'Rally—the Greys!' It was the adjutant, Lieutenant Miller. One or two officers got through to him and troopers forced their way to him as well; he was a big man and he towered above the mass. They formed up again and made another fierce attack on the Russians, slashing and stabbing.

Kinglake said: 'A Scots Grey . . . might have no enraging cause to inflame him, but he was of the blood of those who are warriors by temperament, and not because of mere reason. . . . When numbers of Russians crowded around a Scot of the quality, and beset him on all sides, it did not of necessity result that they had the ascendant. While his right arm was busy with the labour of sword against swords he could so use his bridle hand to fasten its grip upon the long-coated enemy and tear them from their saddles. . . .'

The battle was really won when a fresh squadron of Inniskillings attacked the left flank of the Russians who at this point broke and ran. A little later Sir Colin Campbell rode up and uncovering in salute, he said: 'Greys! Greys! Gallant Greys! I am sixty-one years old and if I were young again I should be proud to be in your ranks.'

I like an incident which took place on the day of Balaklava, when an A.D.C. galloped up to the colonel and said: 'Colonel, ten men who dare go anywhere and know no fear are wanted at once. They have a desperate task to perform. As soon as possible please.'

Colonel Darby Griffiths half-turned in his saddle and spoke to his regiment, in line behind him, 'Greys, from your right, number off.'

It sounds apocryphal, but in fact the incident is authenticated.

The Greys did not serve abroad again after 1856, until the Boer War. The Greys' work in that war was arduous and constant. Exposed alternately to scorching heat and searching cold, the endurance of men and horses was severely tried. If the regiment had no great day such as they had in other wars, they had much success to their credit, despite some sharp reverses. They were present at the relief of Kimberley and the surrender of General Cronje and at the capture of Bloemfontein. The horses suffered more than the men and the horse casualty list is some indication why the days of cavalry were ending; 256 were killed and 507 were destroyed; 465 died, mostly from exhaustion; 2,687 were invalided to sick horse depots and 226 were left on the veldt.

In 1914 during the retreat from Mons—a move made necessary to prevent the complete destruction of the B.E.F.—two squadrons of the Greys were outstanding in holding up a powerful German thrust for four hours, thus giving the infantry time to regroup and take up positions. At St. Quentin some of them charged the Germans, with some men of the Gordons.

Cavalry was little use during that war and after some sharp early lessons many cavalrymen fought as infantry, usually to their disgust. Still, at the important Battle of Amiens in August 1918 the Greys were part of a cavalry brigade held in readiness for the break-through. The break-through came, but the Greys did not take part in the subsequent charge.

After their war service the Greys spent seven years in Egypt, Palestine and India, thus setting a precedent, for the regiment, by tradition, had never before been sent abroad except on active service. In 1938 they were once more back in the Middle East, this time in Palestine to keep the Arabs and Jews apart. They were still there when war broke out.

In March 1941 the regiment was finally and wholly separated from the last of its grey horses and joined the illustrious Eighth Army as an armoured unit. In Crusader, Sherman and Grant tanks they took part in the Battle of Alamein. The following year, in October, they led the way into Naples, and after the Italian campaign they saw service in the invasion of Europe.

They had the distinction—a dubious one, perhaps, in the light of subsequent events—of being the first British regiment to make contact with the Russians when Germany was defeated.

After the war the Greys were back in their old stamping ground, the Middle East, where they trained with Glubb's Arab Legion.

If for nothing else the Greys will always be famous because a woman served in their ranks as a trooper. Her name was Christian Davies (née Cavanagh). Born in Dublin in 1667, she married Richard Welsh. He, without her knowledge, was in some way forced to enlist in a foot regiment, and wrote letters to his wife which never reached her. At last she heard of his being in the Army, so disguised herself as a soldier to go in search of him.

She enlisted in Captain Tichborne's company of foot as Christopher Welsh. In a skirmish before the Battle of Landen she was wounded, and in the next year—1694—taken prisoner by the French, but exchanged.

At her own wish she was now allowed to join the Greys, and continued so until after the Peace of Ryswick. On the renewal of war in 1701, she went back to Holland and re-enlisted in the Greys. She fought at Niuwegen, Venloo, Bonn, and in most of the engagements of the campaign, till at the Battle of Donauwerth she received a ball in the hip, which caused a temporary retirement into hospital. The ball was never extracted, but Christian was again under arms in time to share in the spoils after Blenheim. While forming one of a guard to some prisoners taken in the battle, she again saw her husband after a separation of thirteen years. She lost no time in revealing her identity to him; but so enamoured was she of camp life that she extracted a promise from Welsh that he would pass himself off as her brother.

At Ramillies she was seriously wounded and while she was unconscious and being treated her sex was discovered. This must have caused quite a sensation in the Greys' camp that night.

Lord John Hayes and Brigadier Preston went to see her in hospital and many of the woman's old comrades visited her, too. Lord Hayes sent her 'a parcel of linen' and the Greys' officers contributed to buy her some clothing.

She remained with the Greys, accompanying her husband. She became regimental sutler and was useful in obtaining information; once she and her pack-horse were captured, but released.

In 1709 Richard Welsh was killed at Malplaquet. Christian herself found his body, and was so grief-stricken that she gained the open sympathy of a Captain Ross. This led to her being given the nickname of 'Mother Ross', which stuck to her for the rest of her life. She married Hugh Jones, a grenadier, within three months. In 1710 Jones was killed at the siege of Saint Venant. In 1712 she returned to England, was presented to Queen Anne, and awarded a life pension of 1s. a day. She afterwards went to Dublin and married a soldier named Davies. She died on 7 July 1739, and, at her own request, she was buried among the pensioners in the Chelsea burial-ground. Three volleys were fired over her grave; she was a soldier to the last.

The next year a book was published purporting to be an account of her life and adventures. It is an odd story, and inevitably, rather coarse. According to the writer, not all the members of the regiment were in doubt about the trooper's sex.

The Scots Guards

1660–1713 The Scots Regiment of Guards
1712–1831 The 3rd Foot Guards
1831–1877 The Scots Fusilier Guards
1877–   The Scots Guards

Nickname: the Jocks

THE SCOTS Guards date their existence from 1642, when Charles I commissioned the first Marquess of Argyll to raise a royal regiment. This regiment, intended by the king to be his Royal Guard, became known as the 'Irish Companies', because the regiment had served in Ireland protecting Scottish colonists.

The regiment fought for Charles II at the Battle of Worcester in 1651 and, with others, was scattered in the disastrous defeat. In 1660 Charles landed at Dover and was restored to his throne. He needed an Army and the reraised Scottish Foot Guards became part of it. They were recruited in January 1661 and the Earl of Linlithgow became Colonel, the regiment's third.

The Privy Council records show that five additional companies were ordered to be raised in 1662, but the earliest mention of the regiment in the English State Paper Office is a memorandum on 5 July 1666.

Charles II had apparently been making inquiries about the Scots Guards—wanting them to be brought south in anticipation of a Dutch invasion. The memorandum mentions that the regiment 'corresponds in all things to the King's Foot Guards' (the Grenadier and Coldstream Guards).

The memo adds that the regiment needed a physician and that the men were claiming 1od. a day in pay. The Scottish cavalier, Crichton, writing at this time, says that the Scots were 'not inferior' in social status to the Life Guards—quite a compliment.

Under Colonel James Earl Douglas the Scots Guards declared for William of Orange on his landing. However, the officers remained loyal to James II a little longer and the seceding battalion was actually commanded briefly by a corporal named Kemp.

They fought at Steenkirk in 1692 and were among the regiments which, according to Macauley, were cut to pieces by overwhelming numbers; this was due mainly to the incompetency of Count Sohnes, second-in-command to King William. In reply to urgent requests for reinforcements, the count said: 'Let us see what sport these British bulldogs will make us.' The Guards suffered—but they made good sport for the count while they suffered.

At Namur, 1695, the Guards advanced without firing a shot. Exposed to murderous fire from the enemy ramparts the regiment moved steadily up to the palisades, where they poured in their volleys and drove the enemy back in confusion.

In the early years of the eighteenth century, when affairs in Scotland were critical and with acute friction between England and Scotland, the Guards were often called out to suppress riots in Edinburgh and maintain law and order. In February 1700, a battalion of the Guards was mainly responsible for putting out a fire in Parliament Close and saving Parliament House from destruction. The Treasury gave a special grant of money to the men for their services. It is probably not true that the men had to be cautioned not to start fires in the hope of being paid more money for putting them out.

The Guards were in Spain in 1709–10 and formed part of Stanhope's small force which surrendered in the mountains of Castile after losing 600 officers and men.

In 1712 the Guards were ordered south 'to attend on Her Majesty's person' (Queen Anne). The first battalion—less the Highland company which remained behind until 1714—left Scotland and for 200 years after no detachment of Scots

Guards did duty in their native country. In 1712 the Guards were given the title of '3rd Foot Guards'.

During the forty years between the Flanders campaigns of the 1740's and the French revolutionary epoch the Guards saw a lot of hard service in France and Germany.

At Fontenoy, 1745, the Brigade of Guards (including the Scots) was advancing when they met the French Guards face to face. When within fifty yards Lord Charles Hay of the 1st Guards (Grenadiers) stepped forward with flask in hand and doffing his hat he drank politely to his enemies. 'I hope, gentlemen,' he shouted, 'that you are going to wait for us today.'

The Guards cheered, the French replied and then the fight began; nineteen officers and 800 men of the enemy fell at the first discharge from British muskets.

In 1762, at Brücke Mühle, on the River Ohm, the Scots Guards with other Guards detachments fought so fierce a battle that the bodies of dead men were heaped up to form redoubts. The Guards behaved 'with the greatest bravery', despatches reported, and they lost sixty killed. An incident in the battle was related in the *Gentleman's Magazine* a few years later:

The Foot Guards suffered so severely that the soldiers piled up the dead bodies of their comrades and sheltered themselves behind them as behind a parapet. Thomas Twistleton, the late Lord Saye and Sele, then an officer in the 3rd Guards, at the height of the slaughter reprimanded a sergeant whom he heard utter some expression of horror. The sergeant said: 'Sir, you are supporting yourself on the body of your own brother.' This was his elder brother John, a captain in the Coldstream Regiment, who unknown to him had just been slain.

The Guards saw onerous and unpleasant duty during riots and insurrections, particularly in 1768 when there were demonstrations in support of John Wilkes and a picquet of the Guards had to fire on the mob. A man was killed and this casualty was magnified into 'an inhuman murder by Scottish detachments from the army'. An ensign, corporal and grenadier were tried and acquitted and later the king approved the Guards' actions.

Some of the Guards served right through the American

campaigns from 1776 to 1783. They were especially distinguished at Long Island and White Plains. Three hundred men of the Scots Guards formed part of a composite Guards battalion which, during constant warfare, was never beaten.

And back in Europe in 1793, the regiment distinguished itself at Lincelles by its coolness, steady fire and a magnificent bayonet charge.

In 1801 the Guards were in Egypt. They lost their first men in this campaign in the sea, while making a landing under fire. Their casualties were 200, but they stood firm and with the rest of the Guards brigade were largely responsible for the victory of Alexandria. General Orders record that 'Major-General Ludlow and the Brigade of Guards will accept the thanks of His Excellency the Commander-in-Chief for the cool, steady and soldier-like manner in which they repulsed the attack of the enemy's column.'

It was not long before the Guards were on the Peninsula with Wellington who in 1813 paid a fine tribute—and for Wellington a rare one—to the Coldstream and Scots Guards. 'During the last two years during which the Brigade of Guards have been under the command of the Commander of the Forces, not only no soldier has been brought to trial before a general court martial, but no one has been confined in a public guard.'

About the time of Fuentes d'Onor in 1811, the Guards made themselves popular with the 92nd Highlanders (Gordons). The Highlanders had gone into position very short of provisions, so the guardsmen gave them a ration of biscuits from their own haversacks—a bounty which the Gordons cheered.

The Guards' light companies fought their way into still more history at Waterloo, where, with the light companies of the Grenadiers and Coldstreams, they defended the Château of Hougoumont. It was bitter, sustained fighting—a guardsman's battle. The enemy made a strong attack on the Scots Guards as they retired from a wood on to the great north gate of the château. In the hand-to-hand fighting here, three sergeants, Bryce, McGregor and Fraser, and Private Lister, specially distinguished themselves. Fraser engaged Colonel Cubieres, in command of the French battalion, pulled him from his horse and rode back on it to the court-yard.

[81]

The whole of the French 2nd Corps, 30,000 men, launched attack after attack on the château, but the Guards held out. Wellington referred to the 'utmost gallantry of those brave troops'.

Then, for nearly forty years, the regiment helped to keep the peace in England, Ireland and Portugal.

The gallantry of a new generation of guardsmen was outstanding in 1854, in the Crimea.

At the Alma the Guards advanced to within about thirty yards from a Russian battery firing grape and canister-shot at point-blank range; it took strong-minded men to stand up to that. In addition, a powerful Russian battalion 'was letting drive as hard as they could into us', according to Lieutenant Annesley who lost all his teeth from a bullet in the mouth.

The regiment was forced out of its formation and became something like a huge triangle, with one corner pointing at the Russians. At that point Lieutenant Robert Lindsay (later Lord Wantage) was waving the Queen's Colour, which had its pole smashed and twenty bullet holes through the silk.

Lindsay, in his scarlet coat and gold epaulettes and lace, fearlessly exposed himself so as to rally his regiment; Sergeants Knox and McKechnie and Private Reynolds bullied and coaxed the regiment into formation again. Lord Chewton, too, helped to restore order. Waving his bearskin, he shouted, 'Come on, my lads, we'll beat them and gain the battle!' At this point a ball hit him above the left knee and while in agony on the ground he was severely mauled by two Russians. When the battle subsided he was carried to hospital, where it was found that he had been shot or bayoneted in every part of his body except the left hand and arm. He died on 8 October. Lindsay, McKechnie, Knox and Reynolds won the V.C. Fourteen officers were wounded at the Alma.

At Inkermann the Guards—then about 350 strong*—met a large body of Russians advancing up a slope. Colonel Walker, commanding the Guards, held his fire until the last moment, then ordered the battalion to fire and charge. The Russians,

---

* At the time of the Crimean War the Guards were acknowledged to be one of the finest regiments in the Army. Twenty-nine officers and 935 men went to the Crimea; they averaged 5 ft. 10 in. in height.

not waiting for the bayonet, rolled back down the hill. The Scots were chasing them, when Walker received an order to hold.

Not long after this a column of Russians advanced towards Sandbag Battery and Walker again fired a volley into the mass and advanced with the bayonet. This time the Russians re-treated in disorder as well as with haste and again Walker was ordered to come back. The Russians re-formed and came up the slope again. This time they kept on after the Guards had delivered their volley. Walker gave the order to charge and the Scots drove the Russians down the hill. This time Walker's pursuit was not halted. He is reported to have said later: 'To stop a Scot using the bayonet when his fire is up is a barbarous practice.'

After the Crimea, it was not until 1861 that the Guards again saw foreign service—this time in Canada, at a time when war with the United States appeared possible. However, there was no action and the regiment's worst experience was a near shipwreck at the mouth of the St Lawrence.

In 1882 a battalion of the Guards landed at Alexandria, not far from where their forbears had fought eighty-one years before. A month later they were in action at Tel-el-Kebir, but they were only lightly engaged here compared with their part in the battle of Abu-Klea in 1885. As the British square advanced against the Dervishes the enemy opened fire, but fell back until they reached a gully where 5,000 spearmen lay concealed. When the square was only 400 yards away, this mass of Dervishes rose and charged. The impact hit the heavy cavalry, forced them in and broke the square. The Scots Guards took a major part in the wild hand-to-hand fight that followed and then the Dervishes were driven out and the square closed.

After some action at Hasheen and Tamaai, the Guards returned to England and did not serve abroad again until the Boer War, where they were in action at Belmont, Modder River, Wepener, Diamond Hill, Biddulphsberg and Lombard's Kop, among other places.

In 1901 the Guards took part in General French's drive through Eastern Transvaal and when French left his command in April he paid the regiment a high compliment. 'I have

particularly admired your extraordinary power of marching*
. . . another point which has struck me is the discipline of this
fine regiment . . . you have gone through many hardships and
privations unprecedented in this long and weary campaign . . .
and you have maintained your splendid reputation throughout.'

It is the proud boast of the Scots Guards that during the
Boer campaign no 'untoward incident' marred the record of
the regiment. No Scots Guardsman surrendered himself a
prisoner of war and not a man was unaccounted for on parade
when the rolls were called.

The Guards were among the first to leave for the front in
the Great War, took part in the retreat from Mons and in the
Battle of Ypres. At Loos the final advance of the Guards recalls
the stories of Fontenoy, Waterloo and the Alma. And cut off
at Festubert, a company of the Guards fought to a finish, like
their ancestors at Flodden. At Nonnebosschen Wood they
killed large numbers of Prussians and came out less than a
company strong.

'They die,' somebody once wrote of the Scots Guards, 'but
they are never beaten.'

Between the wars the Guards saw service in Hong Kong,
Canton, Shanghai, Palestine and Egypt. Then came varied and
arduous war service. They were in France and Norway in 1940
and saw further action in North Africa, suffering heavy losses
in the Battle of Gazala, June 1942. They fought magnificently
at Medenine, Tunisia, the following year. Lieutenant Lord
Lyell won a posthumous V.C. for great gallantry on the slopes
of Djebel Bou Aoukaz.

Volunteers from the 2nd Battalion were foundation members of the Long Range Desert Group.

The Guards took part in the bitter fighting on Anzio Beach
and served throughout the Italian campaign of 1943-5. They
fired the last shots in this campaign. Other guardsmen fought
from Normandy to the Baltic, where a small party actually
captured a U-boat!

Since World War II the Guards have served in Malaya,
Cyprus, Egypt and Germany.

* Between April and July one battalion marched 760 miles and were under fire
forty-two days out of a hundred. Another battalion covered forty miles in twenty-six
hours on one occasion.

XI

The Royal Scots

THE ROYAL REGIMENT

1633–1637 Hepburn's Regiment
1637–1653 Le Regiment de Douglas
1653–1688 The Earl of Dumbarton's Regiment of Foot
1688–1751 The Royal Regiment of Foot; also known by the colonel's name
1751–1812 The 1st or Royal Regiment of Foot
1812–1821 The 1st Regiment of Foot or the Royal Scots
1821–1871 The 1st (the Royal) Regiment of Foot
1871–1881 The 1st or the Royal Scots Regiment of Foot
1881– The Lothian Regiment
1881–1920 The Royal Scots (Lothian Regiment)
1920– The Royal Scots (The Royal Regiment)

Nickname: Pontius Pilate's Bodyguard

THE ROYAL Scots (The Royal Regiment) have the longest pedigree of any regiment in the British Army;* it is an extraordinarily impressive record of service. Blenheim is the first name on their long roll of honours, but long before Blenheim the ancestors of the Royal Scots had fought on half the battlefields of Europe.

Their nickname is 'Pontius Pilate's Bodyguard'. The name came into being when they were in the service of the king of France early in the seventeenth century, when the Scots were then known as Le Regiment de Douglas. Le Regiment de

---

* The Coldstream Guards also claim the distinction of oldest regiment. They were in service as early as 1650 and Charles took them with him from Coldstream in 1660 when he marched on London. The Coldstreams, unlike other regiments of the Commonwealth Army, were never disbanded.

Picardy, proud of its ancient lineage, claimed to have been on guard on the night of the Crucifixion.

'Well, if we had been we wouldn't have slept at our posts,' the Scots retorted. 'But as it happens that night we were acting as Pontius Pilate's Bodyguard.'

The Royal Scots, too, are the lineal descendants of those hard and hungry Scots, the Dugald Dalgetties of the north, who flocked to the service of Gustavus Adolphus, King of Sweden. At one time Gustavus had thirteen Scottish regiments in his service; eight of his generals, seventy-eight of his colonels and fourteen of his majors came from the coasts of Scotland.

One of the Scots' first achievements in Swedish service was the capture and defence of Rugenwald in Pomerania. When proceeding to the campaign by sea they were wrecked on the enemy coast. Gustavus was eighty miles away—and those eighty miles swarmed with enemy troops. Colonel Monro, who led the handful of Scots, kept them all day hidden on the shore. At night, wet, hungry and desperate they attacked and carried the town, then held it for nine weeks until Sir John Hepburn relieved them with another Scottish regiment.

Hepburn's Scots captured Frankfurt-an-der-Oder with the bayonet and they won the Battle of Leipzig. They fought for Gustavus in his famous campaigns of 1625–33.

The Royal Scots claim precedence from 26 January 1633. In August that year they arrived, 2000 strong, at Boulogne, for service with the French Army. They were all good soldiers, several French historians point out, reared in the hard school of Gustavus Adolphus and most of them gentlemen.

United with Scottish units from Sweden, Hepburn's men served France from 1635 until 1678, with the exception of three years. With them were ultimately incorporated the representatives of the other Scottish bands which had been in the service of the king of France, so that the Royal Scots can claim some related descent from those fine soldiers of the fifteenth and sixteenth centuries.

A most outstanding soldier, Hepburn took part in several famous actions before his death in action at Saverne in 1636. He was buried in the Cathedral of Toul, where Louis XIV had a magnificent monument built to his memory. It was destroyed during the French Revolution.

The year after the restoration of King Charles II, the regiment of Douglas, as it was then called, and eight companies strong, was brought to England and dates its seniority from that time (1661).

The regiment was afterwards returned to France. In 1666 it was in Ireland and again returned to France. The Scots went over the Alps and took Turin and they fought under the great Turenne against the Dutch. In 1678 the regiment came finally to England. It was first stationed in Ireland; from here four companies were sent to Tangier where they saw much service against the Moors, from whom the Scots captured a standard in 1680.

At the isolated post of Fort Henrietta 164 Scots were cut off; the position was hopeless and their only hope was to cut their way out, but 120 of them were killed on the way.

At this period the regiment had twenty-one companies of a hundred men each. They wore scarlet doublets faced with white, pale grey breeches and hose and plumed hats. The title 'The Royal Regiment' was conferred by Charles II in 1684, when the facings were probably changed to blue. The regiment captured the Duke of Monmouth's standard at Sedgemoor.

The Royal Scots declared for William of Orange. They fought in the campaigns in Flanders and in the subsequent campaigns under Marlborough—at Blenheim, Ramillies, Oudenarde, Malplaquet, Walcourt, Steenkirk, Neer Landen, Namur, Venloo, Schellenberg. They were also engaged at Wynedale, Lisle, Ghent, Tournay, Douai. Down to the Peace of Utrecht in 1713, the regiment played a prominent part.

Steenkirk was an illustrious occasion. The Royal Scots were in the van of this battle and were led by Sir Robert Douglas, who made his name immortal in regimental records. In rapid succession they attacked four French battalions, each placed in depth behind a hedge. The fighting was most severe at the fourth hedge when the Scots were tiring a little and they lost one of their three colours. Sir Robert Douglas ran through a gap in the hedge, killed the French officer who had the colour and threw it back over the hedge to his own men—just as a French marksman shot him dead. A contemporary historian wrote: 'Thus the Scots commander improved upon the Roman general; for the brave Posthumius cast his standard in the middle of the enemy for his soldiers to retrieve, but Douglas retrieved it from the middle of the enemy without any assistance and cast it back to his soldiers to retain.' In this action the Royals and other regiments of the advance guard displayed a determination and degree of valour seldom equalled in military history.

Between 1713 and 1742 the regiment was stationed in Ireland, except for a short tour of duty in the West Indies. The 1st Battalion joined the army in Flanders and fought at Fontenoy. It was brought home in 1745 and was at Culloden. Both battalions returned to Flanders for the campaigns of 1745–8.

The regiment was sent to America during the early part of the Seven Years War; it was at the capture of Louisberg, Cape Breton; in the expedition against Ticonderoga; at the conquest of Canada; at the capture of Dominica, Martinique, Guadaloupe and Havana.

After the peace of 1763 the regiment had spells of garrison duty in Gibraltar and Minorca. These rests did not last long. During the War of American Independence the regiment saw a lot of hard service, including the defence of Brimstone Hill.

One of the Royal Scots' finest fights was at the now forgotten Battle of Lundy's Lane, where 2,500 British troops met 5,000 Americans. The battle raged most of the day and so close was the fighting that at one time the muzzles of the opposing guns were level; an American gun was carried off on a British limber and a British gun on an American limber. The British guns were captured in one American rush, but the Royal Scots recovered them. Not even at Waterloo did the Royal Scots show more courage than at Lundy's Lane.

At the outbreak of the French War, the 1st Battalion went to the West Indies and took part in the harassing warfare of San Domingo, where dysentery, typhus and other tropical diseases reduced the battalion to 123 of all ranks. The 2nd Battalion went to Toulon and afterwards helped to reduce Corsica; it held Elba when the French revolutionary armies were conquering Italy; was in Portugal in 1797, with the Duke of York in Holland in 1799, with Abercromby in Egypt in 1801.

When the French War was renewed the battalion was posted

to the West Indies, where it distinguished itself in the capture of St. Lucia in 1803. In 1806 it was sent to Malacca and then to Madras.

Meanwhile, the 1st Battalion, which had been in England, returned to the West Indies and was present at the capture of Guiana in 1803 and Guadaloupe in 1810. Moving to Canada it served throughout the campaigns of 1812–14, its grenadier company especially distinguishing itself in the hard fighting at Niagara.

Two additional battalions—the 3rd and 4th—had been formed at Hamilton in 1803; the 3rd was present at Corunna and later served throughout the Peninsular War from Busaco to Bayonne. This battalion also represented the regiment at Quatre-Bras and Waterloo. With the 42nd and 92nd High-landers and the 44th Regiment it formed Sir Denis Pack's brigade of Picton's division and was especially noticed for its steadiness in square.

At Quatre-Bras the Royal Scots, with others of the fifth division, under Picton, came 'crushing through the thick green corn, which waved to and fro in the summer wind. . . . A sharp exchange of musketry and the word was given—"Charge!" The Royals . . . fell upon the French like an avalanche and whirled them from the field. Afterwards, un-broken, they received and repelled the thundering charges of Kellerman's renowned cuirassiers.'

The 4th Battalion was sent in 1813 to Stralsund as part of a force to co-operate with the Prince Royal of Sweden in Germany. The battalion remained in garrison in Pomerania for some time and then joined Lord Lyndoch's force before the Battle of Bergen-op-Zoom. This called for a march through northern Germany in the depth of a fierce winter. The 3rd and 4th Battalions were disbanded in the 1820's.

Meanwhile the 2nd Battalion had been in Java, fought in the Mahratta campaigns of 1816–18—including the battles of Nagpore and Maheidpore—and had fought in the first Burmese War. It returned home in 1832. In 1836 the 1st Battalion also came home, after yet more service in the West Indies.

The 2nd Battalion was posted to Canada and served there during the troubles of 1838–9. The 1st Battalion served in the Crimea and fought at the Alma, at Inkermann and at the siege of Sebastopol, where it was joined by the 2nd Battalion.

The regiment took part in the China War of 1860, including the attack on the Taku Forts and the capture of Pekin. After leaving China the 1st Battalion served in India until 1870 and the 2nd Battalion from 1866; in 1878 the regiment was in Malta, then Barbados and South Africa, where the 1st Battalion formed part of the expedition into Bechuanaland and in the operations in Zululand in 1888.

Since then the regiment has seen a tremendous amount of hard service in India, and during the Boer War and the two World Wars.*

Their share in the capture of Orly on 7 September 1914 and their brilliant seizure of the line of the Lawe Canal a month later are feats which will always rank high in the records of the Royal Scots.

One battalion had some incredible experiences during the remarkable but pathetically little known campaign of the River Column in North Russia in 1918–19. In bitter weather they made a drive from Murmansk up the Dwina River and for months were in daily action against the Bolsheviks. For some time they fought, as in the days of Red Indian warfare, from blockhouses in the forests.

Thirty-five battalions of Royal Scots served in the Great War and more than 100,000 men passed through the ranks: 11,162 were killed and more than 40,000 wounded. The regiment won seventy-one battle honours for the war.

Both battalions had early setbacks in the second Great War. The 1st Battalion suffered losses in the German breakthrough. The survivors formed the nucleus of a new battalion, which served in Burma from 1943 to 1945, seeing much fighting. The 2nd Battalion was trapped in Hong Kong and most became prisoners. A new 2nd Battalion fought in Italy and then served in Trieste.

After the war the 1st Battalion served in Hong Kong, Malaya, India and Pakistan. After the amalgamation of the two battalions in 1949 the Royal Scots served in Germany, Korea, Egypt and Cyprus.

With a record like this the regimental motto begins to mean

---

* The 2nd Royal Scots was wiped out in Hong Kong during the rapid Jap advance to the East Indies.

something. It is *Nemo me impune lacessit* (Nobody insults me with impunity).

One of the Royal Scots' finest hours—and one of their most tragic—occurred not in action, but in Scotland itself, one mile north of Gretna, on 22 May 1915. It happened to a service battalion—the 7th—and though this book mostly concerns regular battalions an exception must be made in this case.

On the railway line, standing stationary, was the 6.10 a.m. local from Carlisle. On the same line, approaching from the north—and only a few hundred yards away at 6.54 a.m.—was a troop-train carrying 470 men and twelve officers of the 7th Royal Scots, on their way to active service.

Coming up from the south, at 60 m.p.h. was the Euston-Glasgow express, drawn by two powerful engines. Incredible incompetence and negligence by two signalmen had set the stage for Britain's worst train disaster.

At 6.55 a.m. exactly the troop-train smashed into the local, with such violence that both trains were dragged from the rails, while the engine and leading coaches of the troop-train toppled sideways.

Most of the soldiers were asleep at the moment of impact; some of them never woke again. In the mass of smashed, capsized carriages were scores of men either pinned in so tightly by wreckage or so badly hurt that they couldn't drag themselves out. Within seconds parties of survivors were working feverishly to free their trapped mates.

It was now that the crowning tragedy happened. The Scottish express was thundering up towards the scene. Shouting and waving his arms like a maniac, the driver of the local, who had escaped injury, ran along the rails in a desperate attempt to stop the express.

But it was too late. With a crash heard six miles away, the two giant engines hit the wreckage and ploughed their way into the heart of it, grinding and smashing the already mutilated troop-train to matchwood, thundering through and over the men who were trying to rescue their imprisoned comrades.

Almost instantly, fire broke out. The torn woodwork caught alight from the engines and the flames, fanned by a slight breeze, swept the carriages, incinerating the men in them. Soldier survivors and rescuers from the express were driven back by the flames. They could only listen helplessly to the screams of the dying men. But with furious energy, they set about the task of rescue wherever it was humanly possible. 'They fought their way through the wreckage as though storming a German trench,' an eyewitness said.

Some victims, in agony, begged to be shot; one young officer amputated his own arm to avoid the flames; another soldier, dying, said plaintively: 'If only it had been a fecht!'

Soldiers who had been to the front said that not even in the trenches had they ever seen anything nearly so appalling. 'No words could describe the ghastly horror of it,' a clergyman said.

Almost an hour had to elapse before medical help could arrive on the scene. In the meantime, the Royal Scots survivors, helped by some R.A.M.C. men who had been travellers on the local train, got pickaxes from the battalion tool-wagon and attacked the wreckage. Sailors from the express used crowbars and axes.

Survivors of the ammunition section ran straight to the ammunition wagons, uncoupled them and pushed them to a safe distance from the fire.

First word of the crash was reported by Mrs. Dunbar, wife of the caretaker at the marrying blacksmith's shop at Gretna. Mrs. Dunbar had run across the fields to the crash. Now she hurried back to tell the girl at the post office, who telephoned every surgeon whose name she could find in the Glasgow and Carlisle directories.

There was plenty of work for the doctors and nurses who came hurrying to Quintinshill. Dr. A. Edwards performed two operations under desperate conditions. Two soldiers pinned by the legs cried out to him for help as they saw the wall of flame coming closer. Coolly, the doctor released one man by amputating both legs and the other by removal of one leg only. This man, however, died from shock.

Fire engines arrived from Carlisle, but even with hoses the firemen could not check the flames which raged around the spot where the three engines lay locked together.

The field, converted into a hospital and mortuary, was never forgotten by those who saw it. Every minute stretchers came down the embankment with their grim loads, often only charred bones and flesh. The only trace of many a soldier was a fragment of clothing, a pipe or a pouch, a note-book or a handful of buttons.

For hours the work went on. By mid-afternoon the wounded had all been taken to Carlisle Hospital, the County Hall or private houses. But into the night continued the task of clearing away the wreckage and identifying the dead. Dotted over the field were little heaps of clothing, boots and rifles, equipment and personal belongings.

Pale and dishevelled, grimed and blood-stained, by Sunday the survivors, who had worked unceasingly, were on the point of collapse. That afternoon the Royal Scots called the roll. Fifty-eight men answered their names. More than 200 were dead and 200 wounded, mostly seriously. Another fifty civilians, including children, were also dead.

Few passengers had been on the local and those on the express owed their lives to the two engines taking the brunt of the shock.

In Leith, where most of the troops had lived, Monday was observed as a day of public sorrow; all businesses were closed, all amusements cancelled and the streets were thronged with mourners.

Even a nation engrossed in the bloody struggles going on around Ypres found time to be appalled at the Quintinshill death-roll and to be impressed by the steady discipline and courage of the survivors. The dead were buried at Edinburgh with full military honours, in a common grave seventy feet long. It was an impressive ceremony, but there was an even more moving one in Carlisle.

The little band of soldier survivors, watched by silent crowds, marched through the streets, with grim, young-old faces, all chanting an eerie Scottish song, every fourth line of which ran, 'We shall never, never see them any more. . . .'

XII

The Royal Scots Fusiliers

1678–1707 Colonel the Earl of Mar's Regiment of Foot, afterwards Fusiliers and popularly The Scots Fusiliers Regiment of Foot

1707–1712 The Scots Fusiliers Regiment of Foot; also by the colonel's name

1712–1751 The Royal North British Fusiliers Regiment of Foot

1751–1877 The 21st (Royal North British Fusiliers) Regiment of Foot

1877–1881 The 21st (Royal Scots Fusiliers) Regiment of Foot

1881–   The Royal Scots Fusiliers

The regiment is now amalgamated with the Highland Light Infantry; together they are known as the Royal Highland Fusiliers (Princess Margaret's Own Glasgow and Ayrshire Regiment)

Nickname: the Earl of Mar's Grey-Breeks (very early)

MANY YEARS ago the Royal Scots Fusiliers had a regimental song and this was one of the many verses:

Attention! all ye sodjer lads who love the Twenty-First
And hear one of its gallant deeds in homely rhyme rehearsed
On many a hard fought field, my lad, its laurels have been won
And always true are those who wear the number Twenty-One.

Regiments with songs like this do not crow for nothing and

[94]

the Fusiliers certainly had many gallant deeds and hard fought fields to sing about.

Raised by the youthful Earl of Mar in 1678 and popularly known as 'the Earl of Mar's Grey-Breeks', the Fusiliers began their career as infantry—that is, armed partly with pikes and partly with muskets—but at the end of the seventeenth century they were armed with the fusil, a weapon lighter and shorter than the ordinary musket and equipped with a sling.

The regiment was first employed on active service in the distasteful duty of suppressing the Covenanters. It formed part of Monmouth's victorious army at Bothwell Brig in 1679 and then for the next five or six years detachments of the regiment hunted the Covenanters.

In 1689 the Fusiliers first went on active service—to Holland and Flanders for the campaigns of William III against Louis XIV of France. After minor actions, they took part in the Battle of Steenkirk, 1692, and the following year they were sharply and bloodily involved at Landen. They fought incessantly until 1697 and the coming of peace, but in 1704 they were back in Europe with Marlborough, taking part in all five of his big battles—Schellenberg, Blenheim, Ramillies, Oudenarde and Malplaquet.

The regiment had the great honour of leading the assault at Blenheim, attacking French troops strongly entrenched in the village. The dominant figure on the battlefield that day was Colonel Row of the Fusiliers, who charged at the head of his regiment and fell mortally wounded under the very muzzles of the enemy's muskets.

Lieutenant-Colonel Dalyell and Major Campbell rushed to Row's help and were also shot; other officers were exchanging sword thrusts through the palisades protecting the French. The men made desperate attempts to take the position with the bayonet and when this failed they tried to hack down the palisades. Greatly outnumbered, they lost their colours in a furious enemy cavalry attack, though English cavalry squadrons recovered the colours.

A century and a half later an historian wrote: 'The great breach at Badajoz did not witness a more fiery valour than that of the Fusiliers at Blenheim.'

At Ramillies in 1706 the Fusiliers, with the 3rd Foot (The

Buffs) charged the enemy's left flank at a critical moment and drove three French battalions into some marshy ground where they were nearly all killed or taken.

In the subsequent campaigns of 1710, 1711 and 1712 the Fusiliers were constantly fighting—at Pont-à-Vendin, Douai, Bethune, Saint Vincent and Aire, among other places.

In 1715 the Fusiliers took part in the suppression of the Highland rising and then came a period of comparative in-activity until 1742 when they were once more defending Flanders. At Dettingen, in June 1743, the Fusiliers emblazoned their traditions with another immortal battle.

About midday an officer warned Sir Andrew Agnew, the C.O., that the enemy was on the move.

Agnew said: 'The scoundrels will never have the impudence to attack the Scots Fusiliers!'

To keep his men steady, Agnew ordered the dinner call to sound and himself sat down to a large meal. Not until the enemy began to deploy did Agnew order the drums to sound assembly. When the Fusiliers fell in, Agnew addressed them. 'Lads,' he said, 'ye see yon loons on the hill yonder. Weel, if ye dinna kill them, they'll kill you. Dinna fire till ye see the whites o' their e'en!'

The impenetrable British square had not yet been evolved as a military stratagem and Agnew ordered his regiment to fall back from the centre by right and left. The cuirassiers galloped furiously into the lane thus formed. The Scots fired a volley at them, then charged the horses with the bayonet. The French regiment was practically annihilated. After the battle, the king, George II, said to Agnew: 'Ah, Sir Andrew, the *gens d'armes* got in among you today.'

'Aye, Your Majesty,' Agnew said, 'but they didna' get out again.'

The Fusiliers suffered badly—as did the British Army generally—at Fontenoy in 1745 and soon after this they returned to England to help Cumberland suppress the new rebellion. No sooner was this over than they were back in the Netherlands, fighting at Val.

Belle Isle surrendered to the regiment in 1761. From 1765 until 1781 they were in America; in this campaign they relieved Quebec. Then they spent three years in the West

Indies before coming home.

In 1793 the Fusiliers had an unhappy experience at Martinique. The French royalists of Martinique were being harried by the republicans and they sent messages to Major-General Bruce, commanding British troops in the West Indies, asking for help. Bruce sent the Fusiliers, perhaps because Scots and French had always fought well together. With 800 royalists the Fusiliers advanced to attack the town of St. Pierre. It was then that they found out that enthusiastic amateur soldiers—and especially French ones—could not always be trusted. The royalists were undisciplined; they became confused, fired at one another in panic and so disrupted the plan of attack that General Bruce, not having enough men of his own without the royalists, called off the attack. But the following year, under General Sir Charles Grey, a stronger force, including the Fusiliers, captured the island from the republicans.

In 1804 a second battalion was raised, part of the plan to increase the Army because Napoleon had assembled an invasion fleet at Boulogne. Before its disbandment in 1816 this battalion saw service in Holland, including a ill-fated attempt to capture Bergen-op-Zoom.

In 1807 the Fusiliers were in Egypt, where they suffered severely from ophthalmia—yet another hazard of a soldier's life. Corporal David Brown recorded in his diary: 'I am sorry to say that we had upwards of 200 men blind, some of them in both eyes . . . those who could see a little were put in front and those who could not see took hold of their neighbour's coat-tails until they arrived at the hospital, which was a shocking sight to see.' No doubt Brown was referring to the line of men, but hospitals at this time were also shocking.

In June 1809 the Fusiliers saw plenty of action in the Mediterranean, their chief action being at Messina, Sicily, where they captured many Neapolitan troops. A few years later they helped to capture Genoa, before sailing to America for the war of 1812.

After the victorious Battle of Bladensburg, the Fusiliers were the first to enter Washington, where they helped to burn —under orders—the Capitol and other public buildings. Then followed the Battle of Baltimore, after which the Fusiliers embarked for Jamaica.

In 1814 they took part in the expedition against New Orleans, a dismal affair not only because it was a defeat but because peace between Britain and the U.S.A. had been signed some days before the fight. The Fusiliers were badly mauled and lost one of the most outstanding British soldiers of all time—Brevet Lieutenant-Colonel Rennie. An American historian wrote: 'Colonel Rennie was ordered to storm a redoubt on the American right. He executed his orders with great gallantry and urging forward arrived at the ditch . . . sword in hand he leapt on to the wall, calling to his troops to follow him . . . then he fell. . . .'

General Andrew Jackson referred to Rennie as 'so gallant a soldier', protected his body and ensured that Rennie's watch, ring and brooch were returned to the regiment.

The Fusiliers reached the Continent too late for Waterloo, but they became part of the army of occupation before posting to the West Indies, where at Demerara in 1823 they suppressed a periodic minor rebellion. The grateful inhabitants of the colony presented the regiment with 500 guineas for mess plate, 200 guineas for a sword for Lieutenant-Colonel Leahy and fifty guineas for a sword for Lieutenant Brady, who had especially distinguished himself. Postings to tropical countries were no holiday in those days and during its eight years' service in the West Indies the regiment lost eight officers and 400 men by disease—a terrible price for duty done.

In 1833, after duty at home, the Fusiliers were posted to Australia, where, in New South Wales and Tasmania, they guarded convict gangs—a duty they did not enjoy in the least. In 1839 they thankfully departed for India, where they stayed until 1848.

In August 1854 the Fusiliers were inspected at Cork, preparatory to leaving for the Crimea. Major-General Mansfield, the inspecting officer, moved down the ranks of only three companies, then said: 'That will do, Colonel Ainslee; close your ranks and march past. I never inspected such a regiment!'

In the Crimea morale remained high, but General Mansfield would have been shocked at the physical change in the men after the climate, disease and the Army Commissariat had finished with them. Even so, they were outstanding men.

1. A private of the 43rd (Highland) Regiment, 1742. (The regiment was later renumbered 42nd.) From a sketch in (*Illustrations of the Cloathing of the British Army*), a volume prepared by order of George II

2. The Battle of Blenheim, 13 August 1704

3. The Battle of Fontenoy, 11 May 1745

4. The Black Watch
attacking Fort
Ticonderoga—North
America, 1758

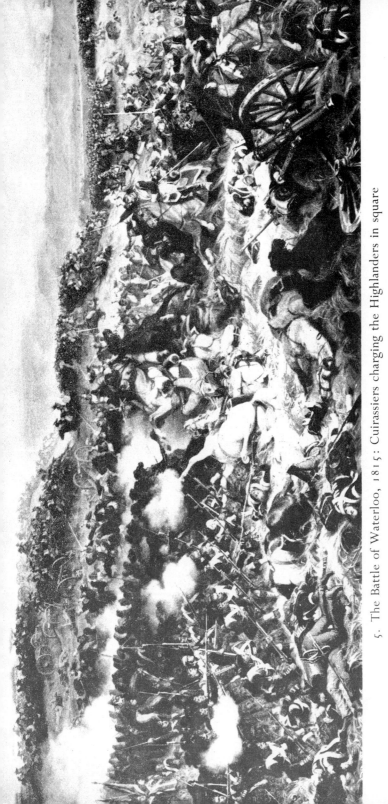

5. The Battle of Waterloo, 1815: Cuirassiers charging the Highlanders in square

6. The defence of the captured Eagle by Sergeant Ewart of the
Royal Scots Greys at Waterloo

7. An attack by Africans on troops commanded by Lieut.-Colonel Fordyce of the 74th Highlanders while forcing their way through the Kroomie Forest, 8 September 1851

9. The 'thin red streak, tipped with a line of steel'. The 93rd Highlanders at Balaklava, 1854

10. The 21st Regiment of Foot (Fusiliers) at the Barrier—Inkermann, 1854

11. The Black Watch attacking mutineers—Indian Mutiny, 1857-8

12. The 93rd Highlanders assault the Shah Nujjif Mosque at Lucknow,
16 November 1857

13. Lieutenant Farquharson of the Black Watch winning the V.C. at Lucknow

14. Officers of the 21st (Royal North British Fusiliers) Regiment of Foot at Barbados, about 1862. The regiment is known today as the Royal Scots Fusiliers

15. The Dargai Heights showing the narrow ridge across which the Gordon Highlanders charged (1897) and where all the casualties occurred

16. A machine-gun post of the 1st Cameronians outside a wood at
Venizel, September 1914

17. The Battle of Bazentin Ridge. An issue of rum to the Black Watch after
the capture of Longueval, 14 July 1916

18. Officers and men of the Gordon Highlanders resting by the roadside near Meaulte, July 1916

19. Roll-call of Seaforth Highlanders on the afternoon of the first day of the Battle of the Somme—Beaumont-Hamel, 1 July 1916

20. A patrol of the 1st Cameron Highlanders in action
among the ruins of Cuinchy, 17 April 1918

21. A Scots Guardsman giving a wounded prisoner a drink
near Courcelles, August 1918

22. A cairn commemorating members of the Black Watch killed in its vicinity on 21 November 1941—about six miles from Tobruk

23. A makeshift officers mess of the Highland Light Infantry just before going into action in the desert, June 1942

24. The 2nd Argyll and Sutherland Highlanders march up to the battle area—France, June 1944

25. Troops of the Royal Scots Fusiliers wait in an orchard for the advance while a barrage is laid down—near Tilley, 26 June 1944

26. The 2nd Gordons outside a German bunker, captured with ninety prisoners, February 1945

27. Men of the Royal Scots after clearing the Japanese out of Payan, January 1945

28. A ceremonial parade of the Royal Scots Fusiliers led by the pipe band, at Tananarive, Madagascar

29. Inscription on a rock in Dongala Gorge, Somalia

30. Cameronians at church parade

31. The scene after the Battle of the Hook, Korea. Here the heavily outnumbered Black Watch stood against the Chinese onrushes and when
ammunition ran out, fought hand to hand

Kinglake wrote: 'The Fusiliers were magnificent troops, men of the finest natural quality, and highly trained.'

They were present at, but not engaged, in the battles of Alma and Balaklava. But they fought in the Battle of Inkermann —'the soldiers' battle'—where their defence of the Barrier and their attacks from it made the regiment even more famous, for the defence of the Barrier meant the success of Inkermann. The outstanding soldier during those six wild and crowded hours was Captain Frederick Haines. Haines, when he became a Field-Marshal, used to say that he would exchange all the other hours of his long life for his six hours at the Barrier. Even today the Fusiliers celebrate Inkermann Day.

The Fusiliers took part, too, in various actions preceding the fall of Sebastopol fortress, including the first of the two bloody assaults on the Redan.

The Fusiliers went to the Crimea with a strength of thirty-three officers and 974 men and received reinforcements of twenty-five officers and 575 men. Two officers and 372 men were killed in action or died in the Crimea, twenty-five officers and 221 men were invalided home.

A new second battalion was formed in 1858 and between this date and 1879 the Fusiliers were in Malta, the West Indies, India, Burma, and the Andaman Islands and Ireland.

In 1879 the 2nd Battalion was in South Africa, fighting the Zulus. They took part in the battle at Ulundi, where the Zulus lost 1,500 of their 20,000 men, the huge black wave of enemy reaching no closer than thirty yards from the British square.

Soon after Ulundi, the Fusiliers stormed, captured and destroyed an isolated hill known as 'the Fighting Kopje', the stronghold of the Zulu chief Secocoeni.

Any hope the Fusiliers might have had of a home posting was dashed by the outbreak of the Transvaal War—the first Boer War—which began in 1880. The Fusiliers garrisoned Pretoria, Potchefstroom and Rustenberg. At Rustenberg, Captain D. Auchinleck,* one of the best and most respected officers who ever served in the regiment, commanded a detachment of sixty Fusiliers. In a fort only twenty-five yards square, Auchinleck, who was twice severely wounded, held the Boers at bay for three months until relieved by a detachment from his own

* As Major Auchinleck he died of wounds in the Burma campaign of 1885.

regiment. This siege, virtually unknown and unrecorded, should have become one of the traditions of the Army.

The four-months' defence of Potchefstoom was no less gallant. Men, women, children, horses and mules were cooped up in a small fort, with a water supply of only nine gallons a day. All but five of the tents were cut up to make sandbags and women and children suffered from exposure. At one time Lieutenant Dalrymple-Hay led a dashing sortie against the Boers, but was unable to find food. When the rations became short the garrison suffered from dysentery, enteric fever and other diseases. In March 1881 with the food exhausted and the sick and wounded dying from hunger the post surrendered, but was allowed to march out with the honours of war.

The larger part of the regiment was besieged at Pretoria and held out for 102 days. Mrs. Gildea, wife of the C.O., won the Royal Red Cross for her work during the siege.

Before the second Boer War, Fusiliers of either the 1st or 2nd Battalion were in Burma, Bengal and Tirah, and took part in several frontier campaigns. The 1st Battalion stayed in India until 1908 and was then posted to Rangoon, where the Fusiliers heard that King Edward had approved of the distinction of 'Martinique' being borne on the regimental colours. The distinction had taken 114 years to come through.

The 2nd Battalion saw much fighting in the Boer War, particularly in Cape Colony and the Transvaal. In recognition of their services in South Africa the Fusiliers were again permitted to wear the white hackle in the sealskin head-dress. This highly valued distinction had been abolished about 1837, to the great distress of the regiment.

Eighteen battalions of the regiment fought during the Great War. The 1st Battalion had a stirring experience in 1914 on their way to Mons, when they crossed the battlefield of Malplaquet. Here the C.O. halted the men and reminded them of the deeds of their regimental forefathers—to some effect, too, for the Fusiliers fought well at Mons.

How well the Fusiliers fought during the Great War is shown by their memorial tablet in St. Giles Cathedral, Edinburgh:

To the Glory of God and in proud remembrance of 319 officers,

23 warrant officers, 928 non-commissioned officers and 4,693 men who gave their lives.

After the war the 2nd Battalion saw service in South Russia, the North-West Frontier of India and in Shanghai, returning home after seventeen years' foreign service. The 1st Battalion was in Ireland and Palestine.

The 2nd Battalion saw intensive action in France in 1940. Their stand near Vimy Ridge helped the B.E.F. to reach the evacuation beaches.

The 1st and 2nd Battalions met in Durban in 1942 and fought together in Madagascar that year. They fought Vichy French, Creoles and Malagaches and by their presence deterred the Japs from a possible attack. Madagascar was no picnic. The fighting was fierce and the Fusiliers had many things to put up with, including stinking swamps, intense heat, insect plagues and the constant depredations of bush rats, which were so aggressive that they even ate Army boots.

After Madagascar the 2nd Battalion saw service in India, Jordán, Palestine and Egypt. It was the first formation ashore in Sicily and among the first in Italy, where the men saw many hard actions. They marched more than 2,000 miles from Italy to the Elbe to take part in the river crossing.

The 1st Battalion saw action against the Japanese in Arakan and Borneo and returned home in 1948 after fifteen years' tough service. That year, too, the 2nd Battalion was disbanded. The 1st Battalion has since served in Malaya and Cyprus.

The Fusiliers' motto was *Nemo me impune lacessit*. On their amalgamation with the Highland Light Infantry this was adapted to *Nemo nos impune lacessit*. It takes brave men to claim such a motto, braver ones to live up to it. The Fusiliers have done so.

XIII

The King's Own Scottish Borderers

1689–1751 Known by the colonel's name; also as The Edinburgh Regiment of Foot
1751–1782 The 25th (Edinburgh) Regiment of Foot
1782–1805 The 25th (Sussex) Regiment of Foot
1805–1881 The 25th (King's Own Borderers) Regiment of Foot
1881–1887 The King's Own Borderers
1887–   The King's Own Scottish Borderers

Nicknames: the Botherers; the Kock-Olly Birds

THE KING'S Own Scottish Borderers (the border referred to is that between the Highlands and Lowlands) got off to a flying start on 19 March 1689, when according to tradition the 800 men needed for its establishment were recruited within four hours; some people said within two hours. This short period seems incredible, but certainly the ranks were full within twenty-four hours.

The regiment's first battle was at Killiecrankie, where it behaved well and set the standard for succeeding generations of Scottish Borderers. In 1691 the regiment was in Ireland and took part in the siege and capture of Athlone, where the Borderers forded the Shannon River under a hail of grape and musketry. At Aughrim it was part of a British force of 18,000 which routed an Irish army of 25,000. After actions at Galway and Limerick, the regiment went to Flanders* in 1692 where

---

* Two veterans of these campaigns, Captain Sterne and Corporal James Butler, were the originals of 'my Uncle Toby' and Corporal Trim in *Tristram Shandy*. Sterne was the author's uncle.

it had some hard fighting, notably at Steenkirk where heavy casualties were suffered, and at Landen.

Next, in 1695, came Namur, where the Borderers learned just how bloody war could be. Namur was strong by nature and had been so strengthened that the town and citadel were considered impregnable. The attack commenced on 18 July and on the 27th the English and Scottish troops assaulted the advanced counter-scarp, which enclosed the great sluice near the gate of St. Nicholas. They were terribly exposed to enemy fire and the enemy exploded a huge mine, which killed twenty-five officers and more than 500 men of the Borderers (then known as Leven's Regiment). Despite this catastrophe, the men rallied and eventually gained a hold on the town, which surrendered on 1 September.

During these campaigns the Borderers had a unique and salutary experience. At this time British bayonets were screwed into the muzzles of the muskets and this action was carried out when the Scots encountered a French battalion, also with bayonets fixed. The Scots were staggered when, at close range, the French poured in heavy musket fire; their muskets had a new contrivance by which the bayonets could be attached to the barrel and still leave it free to be fired. Despite the shock, the Scots rallied and drove the French off.

Nobody knows for sure what the regiment did between its return to Scotland in 1697 and the 1715 Rebellion, in which it took part. Then in 1719 the Scots joined the Vigo expedition before helping to defend Gibraltar against the Spaniards in 1727–8. In 1736 the regiment suffered from one of those frustrating, maddening and apparently senseless War Office decisions—all the privates were drafted to another regiment and sent to Georgia, while the officers and N.C.O.s returned home to raise the battalion afresh.

After service in the West Indies, the regiment fought at Fontenoy in May 1745, where it lost 206 officers and men. Then came Culloden and after that, as if to dim the unpleasant memory, more service in Flanders, including the sanguinary Battle of Val (or Laffeldt).

In 1759 at Minden the regiment was one of six famous British units which repulsed charge after charge of sixty squadrons of the best cavalry in France, routed two brigades of French infantry and swept away a body of Saxon foot—all under heavy artillery cross-fire. 'It was here,' said Prince Ferdinand of Brunswick, 'that British infantry gained immortal glory.'

On 1 August, each year, the Borderers still exercise the privilege of wearing roses in commemoration of the victory; this pretty custom perpetuates the act of the Minden Borderers in plucking roses on their way to the battle.

Minden is noted as being the first engagement in which British troops took aim by placing the butt of the musket against the shoulder and sighting along the barrel. Before this the musket was discharged breast-high in the general direction of the enemy; to take aim was considered unchivalrous.

The Borderers took part in several other battles in this campaign, which was followed by service in Minorca and Gibraltar, where the Scots took part in the closing stages of the famous siege.

In 1793 the regiment turned from land fighting to sea warfare; they became marines. They shared in the glories of 1 June 1794, while a detachment spent five eventful years on board the 98-gun *St. George*, serving at Genoa, Corsica and Elba. These men fought in Hotham's action off Hyeres, captured a Spanish treasure-ship with over a million pounds sterling on board and won high commendation from Earl St. Vincent for putting down a dangerous mutiny of the ship's company in the Tagus.

Between 1793 and 1795 the regiment took part in at least thirteen actions, before posting to the West Indies; they were in action at the island of Grenada.

While on the way to the West Indies one transport was captured by a French corvette, which took the officers aboard. The British planned to take over the corvette, but their plan was betrayed, and they were gaoled on the island of St. Martin. Put aboard another ship, the officers plotted and schemed and finally seized the ship and forced the master to sail to Grenada.

The regiment took part in the action of Egmont-op-Zee, Holland, in 1799, and in 1801 it was in Egypt.

In 1805 a second battalion was raised at Penrith. In this year, too, died Lord Lennox, colonel of the regiment for forty-two years. He was so attached to his men that he pleaded with the king to countermand any suggestion that he be promoted; promotion would have taken him from his regiment. Few commanding officers have been as beloved as was George Henry Lennox.

The 1st Battalion was present at the occupation of Madeira in 1807, after which it sailed to the West Indies, where it fought at Martinique in 1809; it was also engaged at the recapture of Martinique and Guadaloupe in 1815.

After service at home, the Borderers were back in the Indies in 1826 and they stayed there until 1834, mostly in Barbados and Demerara. This was the period of the abolition of slavery, a type of service the Scots could perform with enthusiasm. But, as usual, disease was rife; in 1828 one officer and 110 men died of illness.

Between 1840 and 1868 men of the regiment served in South Africa, New South Wales, Hong Kong, India and Ceylon. Their stay in Madras, 1853, was so outstanding that the Governor issued a special order, reading, in part:

> The exemplary conduct of the 25th Regiment during the period it has been stationed at the Presidency has been specially brought to the notice of the Chief Magistrate, who reports that, while freely mixing with the inhabitants, the men have at all times comported themselves in so peaceable a manner as to have gained the confidence of the natives in a degree that he has never before witnessed, there being no instance of outrage against the person or property by any man of the Regiment since its arrival. There is no better evidence of the real state of discipline of a corps than the steady orderly conduct of all ranks in quarters . . . the Borderers have well maintained the reputation of their distinguished corps.

The 1st Battalion in India in 1878 suffered severely from a cholera epidemic, but at the express wish of all ranks not to be passed over for active service, they were ordered at three days' notice to join the Peshawar Valley field force and took part in actions against the Afghans and Zakka Khels. Later, in Burma, the Borderers took part in expeditions against the Chins and Lushais.

At the time of the great Army reforms of 1881 the Borderers were told that in future their regimental depot would be at York, and not in Scotland, and that they would be retitled 'The York Regiment, King's Own Borderers'. Uproar and vehement protests were immediate. A strong deputation, headed by

Scottish members of parliament, saw the Secretary of State for War, who rescinded the obnoxious orders. It was just another instance of officialdom's ignorance of the value of traditions and *esprit de corps*.

A new 2nd Battalion (raised in 1859) saw sharp service in the Egyptian campaign of 1888, notably in the action at Gemaizah, where the regiment's good conduct and perfect discipline won special mention from General Sir Francis Grenfell.

This battalion went on to even greater things when it formed part of the Chitral Relief Force. At Chitral while the Sikhs were toiling up the slopes, the Borderers, with the Gordons, worked up the centre of the pass. The order for the main assault was given, and the Scots began the ascent. Slowly but surely they made their way up the tortuous and steep hillsides. The Pathans contested every step. Bullets splashed the mud on every side of them, but the Scots stuck manfully to their task, only stopping now and then to haul each other up a more than usually precipitous part of the hill. The first to reach the top of the ridge was Lieutenant Watt of the Gordons. He was set upon by half a dozen Pathans. Two of them went down under his revolver; and then as his men had not yet reached the last ridge he humped down until a fuller rush could be made. Lieutenant Watt had his shoulder-strap carried away by a bullet, which first passed through the brain of a corporal.

A foothold was at last gained on the summit, and the Gordons and the Borderers soon cleared the defenders out at the point of the bayonet. The worst of the fighting was now over, and these two regiments bivouacked on the ground they had won.

The battalion distinguished itself at the taking of Malakand Pass and in the fighting at Swat River and Panjkhora River. In 1897 and 1898 came the campaign against the Afridis in the Tirah.

The Borderers were in action twenty-three times during this campaign. They marched through ice-cold streams, scrambled up precipitous mountains and lived under arduous conditions, constantly under fire by tribesmen. One of their many actions was the first attack on the heights of Dargai.

Major-General Westmacott paid the Borderers a nice

compliment at the end of the campaign. 'I had always heard,' he said, 'that the Borderers were one of the finest regiments in the service. You have been tried very highly. Constant rearguard actions, marching through ice-cold water and then going straight up on the highest hills on picquet duty and fighting all night without either food or blankets; and I have never heard a murmur or an unsoldierlike word. I am very proud of having had the Borderers under my command.'

The 1st Battalion saw continual and rugged service in the Boer War and then again in India. But difficult as these campaigns were, they were picnics compared with the Great War. The Borderers did their share. The spirit which imbued the regiment was well illustrated by Pipe-Major Robert Mackenzie. Mackenzie had long been retired from the Army in 1914, but the thought of action with his old regiment was overpowering, so he re-enlisted. His gallantry and irreproachable conduct made him conspicuous and he was recommended for the D.C.M. Then he fell at Loos—at the age of sixty. By re-enlisting he paid his regiment a high compliment and by accepting him they returned it; reciprocity was always a feature of the Borderers.

During the Great War, the regiment's various battalions lost 359 officers and 6,500 men killed.

In World War II the 1st Battalion took part in the first landing on D-Day and fought throughout the campaign, while the 7th (Service) Battalion was one of the units of the 1st Air Landing Brigade which took part in the gallant but unsuccessful Arnhem landing.

The 1st Battalion went to Palestine in 1945 and served there until the British mandate ended in 1948. This period was one of the most unpleasant and dangerous in the regiment's history, as British soldiers—doing their best to keep the peace—were often attacked and murdered.

The regiment served in Korea. Probably the fighting the Borderers experienced here was the fiercest in their history. At the Battle of Imjin River the enemy was dropping 6,000 shells an hour on their positions. In this fight 'Big Bill' Speakman—6 ft. 7½ in. in height—won a V.C. Actually a Black Watch man, he was attached to the Borderers at the time. He had applied for a transfer to the Borderers but this did not become official until a month after his V.C. action. Second-Lieutenant William Purves, aged nineteen, won the D.S.O. also.

XIV

The Cameronians

SCOTTISH RIFLES

26TH REGIMENT

1689–1751 Known by the names of successive colonels as their Regiment of Foot; also, for a period, as The Cameronians

1751–1786 The 26th Regiment of Foot

1786–1881 The 26th (Cameronians) Regiment of Foot

90TH REGIMENT

1794–1815 The 90th (Perthshire Volunteers) Regiment

1815–1881 The 90th (Perthshire Volunteers) (Light Infantry)

1881 (July–November) The Cameronians Regiment (Scotch Rifles)

1881 (from November) The Cameronians (Scottish Rifles)

In 1881 the 26th and the 90th were amalgamated and became, respectively, the 1st and 2nd Battalions the Cameronians (Scottish Rifles). In 1946 the 1st Battalion was disbanded and the 2nd was renumbered the 1st

Nickname—2nd Battalion: the Perthshire Grey-Breeks

THE ORIGIN of the Cameronian regiment is unique in Army annals, as the regiment is today unique in other ways. The present title—'The Cameronians (Scottish Rifles)'— represents the amalgamation in 1881 of the 26th Regiment and the 90th Perthshire Light Infantry.

When James VII and II withdrew regular troops from Scotland in 1688 his power in that country ended and for some months the Cameronians*—the sect, not the regiment—were masters of the south. Known by various names—United Societies, Society People, Hill Men, Mountain Men—they had maintained throughout the reigns of Charles II and his brother James VII the binding obligation of the National League and Covenant of 1638 and the Solemn League and Covenant of 1643.

In 1680 they renounced allegiance to Charles II and declared war against him and in 1684 they renewed this declaration. This led to their being hunted among the bogs and muirs of the southern uplands. The persecution was fierce, but it did not break the Cameronians' spirit. In the winter of 1688, after the landing of the Prince of Orange they went through the country ejecting various of the clergy from their parishes.

The Prince of Orange had summoned a meeting of the Estates of Scotland to meet at Edinburgh in March 1689, so the Cameronians sent a strong delegation of their own, complete with 500 armed supporters. They protected the meeting for a week until relieved by regular forces, and were offered a week's pay for their services. Typically, the Cameronians rejected the money; they had merely done their plain duty, they said.

The Estates decided to offer the crown to William and Mary and rigid Cameronians objected; they dreaded 'sinful association' with men several of whom not long before had been their persecutors. Even so it was proposed to raise a regiment 'in this juncture of affairs when religion, liberty, country and all were in great danger'.

The Cameronians insisted that in the regiment to be raised the officers should be men of integrity, willing to renew the covenant obligation; that each company should select its inferior officers; that the regiment should choose its own minister, with an elder in each company, and that the military laws against immoral conduct of speech and behaviour should be put into severe execution. It was typical of the Cameronians to want to make conditions and stipulations.

The regiment mustered in May 1689 and again in July, when it had a strength of 1,307. The recruits pledged themselves to

* Named after Richard Cameron, their religious leader.

resist popery, prelacy and arbitrary power—a good Scottish pledge. Each man was required to carry a Bible in his haversack.

The muster rolls are remarkable for the variety of Scottish surnames: Hamilton, Douglas, Oliphant, Cunningham, Johnstone, Muir, Lockhart, Wallace, Allwayes, Bogrie, Dreedan, Glencairn, Hair, Torrokill and many others, including fifty-six 'Macs'.

The regiment was known as 'The Lord Angus' Regiment' (the young Earl of Angus was colonel, but the real leader was the lieutenant-colonel, William Cleland) or 'The Cameronian Regiment'.

Despite their principles—or perhaps because of them—it was not long before the Cameronians were on the verge of mutiny. They complained vehemently of 'profane officers' and of an unnecessary march on the Sabbath; they seemed to regard these complaints more seriously than delay in pay, but pay troubles, at that time, were commonplace.

The regiment had its first fight at Dunkeld and seldom have nearly raw troops been so victorious. Here, 1,200 strong, they fought a force of about 5,000 Highlanders, who a few days before had beaten a combined force of 4,000 English and Dutch. For four hours they fought in street and house and in the market place; when ammunition ran short they tore the lead from roofs and converted it into slugs. At first the Highlanders held the upper hand—literally so, because they fired on the Cameronians from houses overlooking them. The Cameronians retaliated by firing the houses and incinerating the Highlanders.

At last the attacking force drew off, saying that they could fight men but not devils. The Cameronians lost fewer than fifty men; they killed 300 of the enemy and wounded many more. A Jacobite song of the period addressed to the Cameronians, says:

For murders too, as soldiers true,
You were advanced well, boys;
For you fought like devils, your only rivals,
When you were at Dunkeld, boys.

In 1691 the Cameronians were sent overseas for the first

time. Other regiments mocked them for their religious zeal and told them cynically that Flanders was a poor country for Cameronians—there were no hills for them to preach and pray upon. But the regiment held its conventicle and the minister made his usual trenchant attacks on popery.

The Cameronians were so very pure at this time that they petitioned the king against the wickedness of the Army and asked His Majesty to do something about purifying his forces.

Still, their lofty ideals did not make the Cameronians soft soldiers; they pitched in and fought like heroes at the Battle of Steenkirk, where the Earl of Angus was killed; it was his first battle.

The regiment fought at Blenheim, Ramillies, Dendermond, Ath, Wynendale, Oudenarde and Malplaquet. Malplaquet, 1709, was a severe test of courage, for the Cameronians were exposed to a heavy cannonade and suffered losses. 'The soldiers endured it without shrinking, very patiently and with great courage,' the official report stated. Later they took part in the attack on the enemy's centre, an attack which swung the battle.

After service in Ireland, the Cameronians sailed in November 1805 for service in Germany—the ill-fated expedition to the Elbe. Two of the five transports were lost, the *Maria* off Texel with the loss of five officers, 224 men and twenty-two women and children; the *Aurora*, on the Goodwins. All aboard, including nine officers, 250 men and thirty women and children were drowned. It says much for the attraction of the regiment that six months later it was again at full strength.

Later the regiment was in Gibraltar and Minorca and in 1767 went to Canada. At the outbreak of the War of American Independence the Scots helped to defend Quebec; later they were in the fighting at Fort Montgomery and Fort Clinton on the Hudson. They took part in the siege of Alexandria in 1801 and suffered greatly from disease and ophthalmia.

The regiment was with Moore at Corunna in 1808 and later took part in the Walcheren expedition, probably the most disastrous expedition in the history of the British Army. After their ordeal here the whole regiment was classed as unfit for duty. It was sent to join Wellington at Ciudad Rodrigo, but was in such poor shape that the men were withdrawn and sent to garrison Gibraltar. A garrison posting could last a long time in those days; this one of the Cameronians went on for eleven years.

In 1828 they went to India and stayed there until 1841, when they went to China—for the first China War, during which they again suffered terribly from disease. Between 1850 and 1894 the regiment was in Gibraltar, Canada, Bermuda, India, Abyssinia, Malta and India again. The regiment was the only Scottish unit engaged in the Abyssinian campaign of 1864.

One writer said:

The Cameronians are strictly religious and ever act upon that principle, making the war part of their religion, and converting state policy into points of conscience. They fight as they pray and they pray as they fight, making every battle a new exercise of their faith. If they fall in battle they die in their calling, as martyrs to the good cause; they believe that in shedding their blood they finish the work of their salvation. From such maxims of faith the Cameronians may be slain but never conquered. Great numbers of them have lost their lives but few if any have yielded. Whenever they believe their duty or religion calls them to it . . . they are always ready to encounter hardships . . . and bravely rush on to death or victory.

Men like these are hard to defeat.

Significantly, after the Cameronians had been well and truly blooded they gave up trying to reform the soldiery. They never did lose their idealistic zeal but after about twenty-five years they were as normally sinful as any other regiment of the line. Between 1689 and 1900 the Cameronian battalions were engaged in fifty-three major campaigns and battles.

Most Scottish regiments have interesting customs, but one practised by the Cameronians is particularly intriguing. When at divine service in camp or in the open the regiment sends out picquets under officers to scout the country and give the all clear for the service to proceed. This custom stems from the bad days during the 1680's when the Cameronians—then not a regiment but the followers of Richard Cameron—were forced to hide in the trackless country of the Southern Uplands. Here they held their services as usual but for their own protection against the king's troops they posted picquets to give warning of their approach. For much the same reason the Cameronians carry rifles to church and even into church where rifle racks are provided; and they do not have music to and from church.

The 90th Perthshire Light Infantry, destined to become 2nd Battalion Cameronians, had as fascinating a beginning as the senior regiment. The 90th owed its being to the remarkable Thomas Graham, Laird of Balgowan, a civilian without military training.

In 1791 Graham took his ailing wife to the south of France, where she died. He was taking her body back to Scotland when, at Toulouse, a drunken mob of municipal guards and volunteers seized and opened the coffin, claiming that it held contraband. This outrage so angered Graham that he swore vengeance—and being naturally a mild-mannered man his vow was all the more intense.

He served at the siege of Toulon as a gentleman volunteer, quickly learned something about soldiering and on returning to England asked to be permitted to raise a regiment at his own expense. The king disliked the idea of giving a military command to a civilian, but he granted Graham's request. Graham gave neither the king nor the British Army cause to be sorry for the decision, but for fifteen years he remained a mere honorary colonel, without permanent rank or pay. Not until 1809, after much distinguished service, was Graham gazetted as a major-general on the regular list. As a Scot, Graham had a fine martial sense and in time he became Lord Lynedoch, a well-deserved distinction. His big moment came at the Battle of Barossa, in 1811, when he was sixty years old. He was in command of all British forces engaged and he led them with heroic, inspired vigour.

His regiment, the 90th, served in the Quiberon expedition, at the occupation of Isle Dieu and in garrison at Gibraltar. In 1798 it was at the capture of Minorca. While in camp here, the 90th's system of simple and practical light manoeuvres attracted the attention of Sir John Moore; the general later introduced these manoeuvres to his illustrious Light Division. Temporarily under command of Colonel Rowland Hill, the 90th, wearing helmets, as a light infantry unit, was mistaken by the French for dismounted cavalry—and therefore a relatively easy target. The French cavalry charged down on the Scots, who stood cool and calm until the Frenchmen were fifty yards away. Then, by well directed fire, they broke the charge completely; only a few French reached the line and they were bayoneted.

The regiment went to the West Indies in 1805 and spent some years in Antigua; it was engaged in the capture of Martinique in 1809 and Guadaloupe in 1810. Later it was in Canada, Malta, the Ionian Islands and Ceylon from 1835 to 1846. The regiment was busy putting down disturbances but it had some of its own, caused by the climate, which the Scots did not like.

The name of Private Gunnion lives in regimental records for unusual bravery when the regiment was on the way to South Africa in 1846. The transport *Maria Somes* was badly battered by a storm in the Indian Ocean and lost her rudder. Gunnion volunteered to dive and replace the rudder; he had to make many dives and was in constant danger of being attacked by sharks. On the next trip, too, the ship was damaged and Gunnion dived repeatedly into greasy, murky water in the ship to close a sea-pipe so that the ship could be pumped out.

The regiment served at Balaklava and took a leading part in the siege of Sebastopol; on the day of the taking of Sebastopol the 90th sent in a blank sick report, although, in fact, many of them were very ill indeed. No man wanted to miss the fight, but 282 of them missed the trip home; they stayed in the Crimea. A 90th subaltern in the Crimea was Garnet Wolseley, later to become Field-Marshal Viscount Wolseley, V.C.

Next came the Mutiny. Part of the regiment arrived earlier than the other at Calcutta and was in time to take part in the attempt of Havelock and Outram to relieve the Lucknow Residency and was itself shut in. The other wing of the 90th took part in Colin Campbell's successful relief; the two parts of the regiment met in Lucknow's square of Motee Mahal, where there were 'ecstatic reunions'. Fighting in the Mutiny was fierce and the climate severe and 300 Cameronians were killed. That the regiment won six V.C.s in this campaign is proof enough of its battleworthiness.

The old regimental song put it succinctly:

In Havelock's fights and marches, the Ninetieth was there,
In all the gallant Ninetieth did, your Robert did his share;
Twice he went to Lucknow, untouched by steel or ball,

And you may bless your God, old dame, Who brought him
    safe through all.

The 90th remained in India until 1869 and went to the Cape
in 1878 for the Kaffir War, fighting at Kambula and Ulundi
with its usual cool and soldierlike conduct. There followed
another fifteen-year tour of duty in India, and then the Boer War.

Thomas Graham would have been proud of his battalion in
the Great War, and sad for them, too, especially at Neuve
Chapelle where it advanced against uncut barbed wire and
despite appalling losses carried its objective. When relieved,
three days later, one young officer was on his feet and about
150 of the 900 other ranks who had gone into action.

The regiment has always been proud that one of its service
battalions—the 7th—was the last unit to leave Gallipoli at the
now famous evacuation.

Battalions of Cameronians fought and died, too, in
Macedonia, Palestine, Egypt and Mesopotamia. Few people
realized how much they had sacrificed until their memorial
was unveiled in Glasgow in 1924; it commemorates 7,074
Cameronians dead.

After the war Cameronians of one battalion or the other
served in Ireland, China, India, Iraq and Palestine.

In World War II many men of the 2nd Battalion were
evacuated from Dunkirk. This battalion later saw service in
Madagascar, Iraq, Sicily and Italy, where the fighting was particularly fierce. After a spell in Syria, the 2nd Battalion was
sent to North-West Europe and was in at the death.

The 1st Battalion served in the Far East and came out of the
1942 Burma campaign only three platoons strong. Brought up
to strength, they saw hard fighting under dreadful conditions
in 1944 and were again reduced to 'a gallant little band'.

After the war the Cameronians served in Bahrein, Kenya,
Jordan and Malaya. This was where they saw their toughest
postwar service, in the arduous and hazardous work of chasing
bandits. One soldier, writing home, described it as 'a sort of
field sport'. Then, more soberly, he added: 'God willing, I
will be home next month.'

'God willing' was the way the Cameronians always looked
at everything.

XV

The Black Watch

ROYAL HIGHLAND REGIMENT

42ND REGIMENT

1725–1739 Independent Companies

1739–1751 The Highland Regiment of Foot; also by the colonel's name

1751–1758 The 42nd Regiment

1758–1861 The 42nd Royal Highland Regiment of Foot

1861–1881 The 42nd Royal Highland (The Black Watch) Regiment of Foot

73RD REGIMENT

1758–1762⎫
1779–1786⎭ The 2nd Battalion 42nd Royal Highland Regiment

1786–1809 The 73rd Highland Regiment of Foot

1809–1862 The 73rd Regiment of Foot

1862–1881 The 73rd (Perthshire) Regiment

In 1881 the two regiments became, respectively, the 1st and 2nd Battalions the Black Watch (Royal Highlanders). In 1934 the title was changed to The Black Watch (Royal Highland Regiment). The 2nd Battalion was disbanded in 1948, re-raised and in 1956, again disbanded

Nickname: the Forty-Twa

OF ALL Scottish regiments, Highland or Lowland, the Black Watch has become the best known and has been called, with some justice, Scotland's favourite regiment. The very name of the regiment has an evocative ring; there is something

[117]

gallant about it, something dashing and infinitely martial.

It was 'black' because of its dark tartan (black, green and blue); it was 'watch' because the men were employed to keep watch—and the peace—in the Highlands. This simple origin of the name has long since been forgotten; the name itself remains to remind us of the quintessence of valour.

When the Black Watch was formed it had among its officers seven Campbells, four Munros, four Stewarts, three Grants and one Fraser. The same families have officered it ever since and have supplied more than 275 regular officers apart from wartime appointments.

From 1725 until 1739 the Black Watch was not a regiment, but six independent companies. When they were regimented in 1739 they were under the Earl of Crawford and Lindsay, a Lowlander. Though of different clan origin they wore a uniform tartan which has since become known as the Black Watch tartan.

At one time George II, having heard much about 'these Scot soldiers', ordered that three privates be sent to St. James's Palace for his inspection. Fine strong, proud men they performed the Manual and Platoon Exercise for him and George was greatly impressed—so impressed that he gave each man a guinea. The Black Watch men took the tips, but on the way out they handed the money to the porter. History does not record what impression this magnificent gesture made on George. One of the soldiers was Private John Campbell, who, as a captain, was killed at the Battle of Ticonderoga (America) in 1758.

The 42nd was at Fontenoy and was mentioned for its 'extraordinary gallantry' at Ticonderoga.

A second battalion, formed in Perthshire, went to the West Indies and after service there it was posted to Lake Ontario, where it served until the final capture of the Canadas in 1760. In 1862 it was amalgamated with the 1st Battalion.

After service in Cuba the battalion was employed for years in harassing service against the Indian tribes; it particularly distinguished itself at Bushy Run in July 1763.

The regiment came back to Cork in 1767, but when the War of American Independence broke out it was again sent to America. Just before sailing the regiment had a strength of 921

Highlanders, seventy-four Lowlanders, three English, one Welsh and two Irish soldiers. It fought at Long Island, White Plains, Brandywine, Charleston and other places and enhanced its reputation by its valour at the storming of Fort Washington and at the defence of Pisquata.

'No regiment,' a memo of the time read, 'was exposed to more danger or underwent more hardship or suffered more from both.' The 2nd Battalion, raised again in 1779, had been fighting in the East Indies.

One of the most distinctive features of the Black Watch uniform is its red hackle, a flaming feather which adorns the left of their feather bonnets. According to legend, the regiment won the right to wear the red hackle on 1 January 1795 at Guildermalsen in the Low Countries campaign.

This campaign was an arduous one. The regiment fought in bitter cold up and down the Rhine and made forays across its frozen waters. Main centres of the fighting were Nijmegen and Arnhem, where men of the same battalion were to see battle 150 years later.

When the regiment returned home later in 1795, an issue of red feathers, probably vulture feathers, was made on parade. In 1822 an Army order made official the regiment's right to its Red Vulture Feather. Some time after this somebody started the story that the feathers had been taken away from a regiment accused of cowardice at Guildermalsen and given to the Black Watch. This was not true. The regiment believes that the custom derives from the long years spent in America.

The regiment saw further service in the West Indies at St. Lucia and St. Vincent. It was at the capture of Minorca in 1798, at Genoa, Cadiz and Malta and then it won undying fame in Egypt in 1801. The Black Watch, brigaded with the 28th Foot (Gloucesters) defeated a French force known as the Invincibles.

Referring to this battle, an historian wrote: 'The 42nd Regiment stands pre-eminent for gallantry and steadfastness which would be difficult to match in the history of any army.'

There seemed hardly a year when the Black Watch was not serving somewhere. In 1805 it was in Gibraltar and then, in December 1808, took part in the awful retreat of Corunna, marching shoeless across mountains deep in snow, starving and ragged, but disciplined. On 16 January 1809 they faced a vastly superior French force at Elvina. Sir John Moore shouted: 'Highlanders, remember Egypt!' The 42nd fired a volley and followed up with a bayonet charge, driving the French before them. The Black Watch, though, lost six officers and 140 men.

Then came a series of famous battles: Salamanca, Burgos, Pyrenees, Nivelle, Nive, Orthes and Toulouse. At Toulouse on 14 April 1814 General Pack rode up to the regiment and said: 'General Clinton has granted my request that in the charge which we are about to make on the enemy's redoubts the 42nd shall have the honour of leading the attack. The 42nd will advance!'

It was another bayonet charge, in which the 42nd gloried; they took the heights, but lost heavily doing so.

During the Peninsular campaign the 42nd had been taken out to serve—and suffer—in the Walcheren expedition. Another 2nd Battalion, raised in 1802, fought at Busaco, Fuentes d'Onor and Ciudad Rodrigo; it was merged with the 1st Battalion in 1812.

The 42nd fought its way still further into history at Waterloo. One famous incident concerned a sergeant who went forward to retrieve the colours from a dead regimental standard-bearer. He held the colours so fast in death that the sergeant could not loosen his grasp in time to avoid the advancing French. Desperate, he hoisted the dead man, colours and all, to his shoulders and carried them back to his own lines. The French clapped and applauded the almost herculean feat, although, in those days, to miss so narrowly taking an enemy standard was a bitter disappointment.*

Then came service in Gibraltar, Malta, the Ionian Islands, Bermuda and Nova Scotia. It was very much a case of 'Join the Black Watch and see the world'.

The regiment was present at the Alma and at Balaklava and Sebastopol.†

The day before the Battle of the Alma, the Black Watch

---

* A similar story is told about the Royal Scots. Perhaps only the one incident was somehow credited to both regiments.

† In one of the battles Private Campbell was killed by a cannon-ball which entered his abdomen. When the body was raised for burial after the action the shot bulged out of the skin at the back. The spine was smashed to pieces but the ball, weighing 24 lb, could not get through this tough Scot!

arrived at the Bulganak River, gasping and fainting with heat, thirst and weariness. Kinglake notes 'that the stern discipline of Sir Colin Campbell would not allow even the rage of thirst to loosen the high discipline of his splendid Highland regiments. He halted them a little before they reached the stream and so ordered it that . . . they gained in comfort and knew they had been the gainers.'

When the time came for the Highlanders to charge matters were serious, and twelve battalions of enemy faced the three of the Highland Brigade. Campbell made a short address, which wound up: 'Now, men, the Army is watching us. Make me proud of my Highland brigade. Be steady . . . silent . . . fire low. Forward the 42nd!'

He was an inspiring leader; he knew, as Scottish leaders have always known, how to get the most out of his men. 'Smoothly, easily, and swiftly the Black Watch seemed to glide up the hill . . . now their plumes were on the crest. A few deadly volleys and the Russians fled in confusion, followed by the exulting shout of the triumphant Scots.'

The regiment was home for only a year before sailing for India—and the Mutiny. It fought at Cawnpore and at the siege and capture of Lucknow, with its many associated actions.

The Scots have at least one trait in common with the Australians; when their officers and N.C.O.s are out of action there is always a private soldier to take command.

During the blackest moments of the Indian Mutiny one company of the 42nd stationed at Sissaya Ghaut held thousands of Sepoy rebels, who repeatedly attacked the Highlanders. Eventually every officer and N.C.O. was either killed or so badly wounded as to be forced out of action.

In this crisis two privates, Cook and Miller, took command. Under heavy enemy fire they gave orders and encouraged the men. A contemporary historian wrote: 'These two men directed their comrades and exhibited courage, coolness and discipline in such a manner as to command not only the admiration of all who were present, but of the whole Army.'

The Black Watch detachment beat back the Sepoys. Cook and Miller were promoted in the field; one of them was later commissioned. Both received the V.C.

The 42nd served in the Ashantee expedition, under Wolseley. Wolseley later was to write:

> For the honour of breaking through the masses of the enemy that crowded the road leading to King Koffee's capital, I selected my best battalion, the Black Watch. No finer body of men, with more gallant officers, or under a better or more determined leader than Colonel McLeod, were ever sent upon such a mission. Rait's guns raked the road with a heavy shell fire, whilst volley after volley of musketry must have slain hundreds, and thus helped to open a path for those splendid Highlanders. The orders I gave Colonel McLeod were to disregard all flank attacks as much as possible, and to push forward straight for Koomassee. . . .
>
> It was inspiring to see this distinguished Scottish gentleman sally suddenly forth from the village at the head of his historic Highlanders, their pipes playing the old war-like music of Scotland, all ranks knowing full well that come what might they must sleep that night at Koomassee or die on the road to it. Many ambuscades were encountered and each taken with a rush, for what were such obstacles to men like those of the Black Watch! They were from the first moment, as they pushed forward from Ordahsa, met with a terrific fire; many fell wounded, but nothing could stop them. The Ashantees seemed at last to realize this, for the shouting in front ceased for a moment as they fled in all directions in wild confusion. . . .
>
> Just before I entered the city Sir A. Alison had drawn up the troops on a wide open place in the city where he received me with a general salute. . . . All ranks felt they had done a brilliant day's work, and for our victory I am sure many fervent thanks went up to God that night.*

After Ashantee came Egypt and the Nile campaigns, during which one of the 42nd's finest battles was Tel-el-Kebir, 1882. The commander-in-chief decided to make a night march against Arabi's position at Tel-el-Kebir, and to assault it in the dawn. On the night of 12 September the force of 17,000 men set out across the desert, leaving its camp-fires burning. The 1st Division under General Willis was on the right, while on the left was Hamley's 2nd Division, including the Highland Brigade. Between the divisions was the artillery, and in the rear on the right flank was Drury-Lowe's cavalry. As a guard on the extreme left moved the Indians with the 1st Seaforth Highlanders.

The Egyptians thought the British fast asleep at Kassassin, but they were massed at Ninth Hill in the dark about five and a half miles from the trenches. Soon the whispered word was

---

* H. M. Stanley saw the battle. He wrote: 'The audacious spirit and true military bearing of the 42nd challenged admiration.'

given, and the men, rising from the sand, stood ready. Silently the column slipped away into the Egyptian night, and was soon swallowed up in the blackness. Over endless sand went the men in attack formation with not a light showing. Not a rattle came from the deadened wheels, and the silence was broken only by the occasional coughing of a horse or muttered order passed from rank to rank. The shadowy lines moved ghost-like over the sand, stealing nearer and yet nearer.

Every man knew that the end was to be a mighty rush, and for five hours in that gloom the weird silence of the moving multitude fascinated every man in it. In the grey gloom ahead lay the trenches, and timed to the minute the force advanced to them unseen and unsuspected, covered by the mists of early dawn. In double lines the brigades drew to within 400 yards just as the first glimmer of day appeared.

Suddenly a challenge rang out and a bugle blew. The enemy sentries had seen. The next instant the trenches belched forth with a line of flame which lighted up the phantom columns and sparkled on the bayonets. The order to charge was given and the foremost British lines rushed forward. The enemy opened artillery fire on the leading lines but in seconds the Highland Brigade, the 42nd leading, was over the ditch and scaling the parapet. High on the earthwork the pipes sounded and the Black Watch men were bayoneting right and left. The rest of the Highland Brigade and the Irish stormed in at the same time along the line, and in twenty minutes the enemy was in full flight. The British guns now passed at the gallop, the gunners calling out to the Black Watch, like the Greys at Waterloo, 'Scotland for ever!'

The rush of men out of the night had had a terrifying effect, and the enemy hordes collapsed. Arabi Pasha was pursued by cavalry, taken in Cairo, and then exiled for life. The battle, which raised Wolseley to the peerage, cost the British 339 men, out of which 240 were of the Highland Brigade, to whom Alison shouted, 'Scotland will be proud of the day's work!'

At Kirkeban, three years later, the regiment stopped the rush of the enemy, held them and waited for the inevitable order: 'Black Watch, forward! Charge!' With pipes playing, the Highlanders drove the enemy over the ridges of rocks at the point of the bayonet.

After Egypt the Black Watch saw service in Mauritius and India before joining the army for the Boer War, in which they suffered terribly at Magersfontein. Then came the two Great Wars and more active service. The 42nd did its part.

The 1st Battalion Black Watch took part in the retreat from Mons, the first Battle of Ypres where it lost twenty-nine officers and 478 other ranks, and the Battle of Loos, and was engaged right through the war until the tremendous defensive battle of the Lys.

After service in India and the Sudan, the battalion again saw service in France. Re-formed after Dunkirk, it went later to the Middle East, fought at Alamein and from then on was engaged in every major action of the campaign. Later the battalion was the first to set foot on German soil.

The 73rd had almost as eventful a career as the 42nd. After its embodiment in 1780 (as 2nd Battalion Black Watch) it sailed for India; seven and a half companies were afloat for thirteen months and thirteen days before they reached Bombay—a hardly inspiring start for the regiment.

The battalion served against Hyder Ali and his son Tippoo in 1782-3; they were probably the most serious enemies the British ever faced in India. The battalion was in garrison at Mangalore when Tippoo invested it. It was an astonishing defence: 250 white troops and 1,500 natives held at bay Tippoo Sahib's army of 90,000 for nine months.

It was at the siege of Pondicherry, the capture of Ceylon (1785) and the storming of Seringapatam.

Between 1810 and 1814 the regiment saw garrison service in New South Wales, Tasmania and Norfolk Island—a duty which displeased them very much.

A second battalion of the 73rd was, during this period, fighting on the Continent, climaxing its efforts with a fine performance at Quatre-Bras and Waterloo; twenty-two of its twenty-three officers were killed or wounded. In square it resisted no fewer than thirteen charges by cuirassiers.

The 73rd travelled to Ceylon, elements of it via New Guinea, New Britain and the Moluccas. It took part in the Kandyan (Ceylon) War of 1815-17.

It saw service in Gibraltar, Malta, the Ionian Islands, Nova Scotia, Canada, Montevideo; it fought in the Kaffir Wars of 1846–7 and 1851–3. In mid-winter of 1852 the 73rd made a forced march carrying two blankets and greatcoats, seven days' biscuits and groceries and seventy rounds. There was some complaining among the men, who said they could not march much further carrying this load. The C.O., Sir William Eyre, liked complaints no more than any other Scottish commanding officer. 'We will relieve you of the necessity of carrying such a heavy load,' he said—and burned the blankets of sixty of the worst grumblers. According to one writer in recent years, the 73rd never again complained about anything.

As a single battalion unit, the 73rd was on the Nepal frontier in 1858–9 and eventually returned home in 1861.

After five years, the battalion went abroad again and stayed away for fifteen years—in China, Ceylon and India. In 1786 the regiment had become the 73rd and it was not until 1881 that it reverted to its original position of 2nd Battalion Black Watch.

The battalion was in India when the First World War broke out, but returned to France for the fighting at Givenchy, Neuve Chapelle, Festubert and Loos. After Loos the battalion was sent to Mesopotamia and was soon in action at Sheikh Sa'ad with orders 'to attack where the fire is thickest'. They occupied Baghdad and later saw more fierce fighting, sharing in the attack of April 1918 when the Turkish armies collapsed.

The battalion was part of the Occupation Force in Germany, had service at home and later went to Palestine, where it did some thankless bandit-busting.

Late in 1940 the Scots were rushed to Berbera, via Aden. Here, for two weeks, they were in action against the Italians; then they were taken back to Aden. The battalion regarded the brief expedition as a holiday and went back to the Middle East refreshed.

In Crete in 1941 an officer of the 2nd Black Watch diligently studied signals sent by German troops to their supply planes and by copying these signals he managed to acquire some very useful supplies. His battalion, in October of that year, was sent into Tobruk by sea to help the Australians in their defence of that besieged town.

At one time during the war a Black Watch battalion was doing garrison duty at Gibraltar and how seriously they took their duties may be gauged by this incident. A Jock sentry saw a civilian acting suspiciously—he seemed to be looking too closely at military installations—so the sentry arrested the man who was put in a cell in the guardroom. The civilian protested vehemently and said that he was General Eisenhower.

'Then why the civilian get-up?' the guard-commander asked him.

'Security reasons,' the doubtful character said. 'I can't afford to have my identity known.'

This amused the guard-commander. 'I bet you can't!' he said.

Still, he reported to a higher authority that the civilian he had arrested was very annoyed and some hours later inquiries reached a climax when some top brass rushed to the guardroom and ordered the man's release. It happened that he really *was* General Eisenhower.

When he got over his annoyance Ike treated his arrest as a joke—much to the relief of the officer of the guard.

The Black Watch served in Korea, too, where it soon became proficient in the new type of all-in warfare which developed in that war. Not that it was so different from trench warfare of 1914–18, but it was new to the soldiers of 1952.

The Black Watch's principal action was at the Hook, key to the Samichon Valley leading to Seoul, the capital. On the night of 18 November 1952, when the battle took place, there were eighteen degrees of frost. After preliminary artillery bombardment, the Chinese made a determined assault on the Black Watch position. 'A' Company was attacked from three different directions, the enemy advancing with his own mortar and artillery fire and sometimes in front of it.

About ten-thirty the Hook was reported clear of enemy, but heavy shelling began again and after midnight the enemy attacked fiercely again and made some progress, but the Black Watch held firm during a night of particularly hard and confused fighting, in which many a Scot—in 'A' Company especially—used a spade as a weapon when his ammunition ran out.

Constantly the Black Watch men retired to their tunnels on

the hillside and called for their own artillery to shell the position—evidence of cold-blooded courage. By four-thirty the Scots were mopping up and by six-thirty they had cleared the Hook.

A feature called Black Watch Hill is a standing memorial to the battalion's courage and stamina during its thirteen months in Korea.

The Black Watch was specially chosen to go to Kenya in 1954 to fight the vicious Kikuyu bandit gangs of which the Mau Mau were the vilest. The Jocks took this duty very seriously and eventually mastered the marauders.

No account of Scottish soldiers would be complete without reference to Sergeant Donald MacLeod, one of the most remarkable of Black Watch men. A sergeant at seventeen, MacLeod saw action at Schellenberg, Blenheim and Ramillies and became the champion swordsman of his regiment, an extraordinary distinction at a time when every soldier could use a sword.

MacLeod fought and beat a French officer and a French sergeant and a German officer. Then he was to meet an enormous Irishman named McLean. The two men shook hands before the contest and McLean squeezed the Scot's hand fiercely, hoping, apparently, to disable it. All he did was to irritate MacLeod, who fought with such aggressiveness that he cut off the Irishman's right arm.

He was wounded at Sherriffmuir and again at Fontenoy. He transferred to Fraser's Highlanders and saw more action at Louisburg and Quebec. It was in MacLeod's plaid that Wolfe was carried off the field.

Although now over seventy years of age, MacLeod guarded Wolfe's body on the journey to England. Not yet through with soldiering, MacLeod went to Germany with Campbell's Highlanders and was wounded twice more. He was eighty-eight and still serving when he retired, but before he died, at the age of 103, he had other adventures including a shipwreck. During his seventy-one years' service, MacLeod took part in six major battles and innumerable smaller ones and he was wounded four, possibly five times.

XVI

The Highland Light Infantry

CITY OF GLASGOW REGIMENT

71ST REGIMENT
1777–1786 The 73rd (Lord Macleod's) Highlanders
1786–1808 The 71st (Highland) Regiment of Foot
1808–1809 The 71st (Glasgow, Highland) Regiment of Foot
1808–1810 The 71st (Glasgow Highland Light Infantry)
Regiment
1810–1881 The 71st Highland Light Infantry

74TH REGIMENT
1787–1816 The 74th (Highland) Regiment of Foot
1816–1845 The 74th Regiment of Foot
1845–1881 The 74th (Highlanders) Regiment of Foot

In 1881 the two regiments were amalgamated as the Highland
Light Infantry, the 71st becoming the 1st Battalion and the
74th the 2nd Battalion. In 1923 the title was changed to The
Highland Light Infantry (City of Glasgow Regiment). In 1948
the regiment was reduced to one battalion. In 1959 the
Highland Light Infantry and the Royal Scots Fusiliers com-
bined to form a new regiment, the Royal Highland Fusiliers
(Princess Margaret's Own Glasgow and Ayrshire Regiment)

Nickname: the Pig and Whistle Light Infantry

THE H.L.I. has the distinction of a longer roll of battle
honours than any other regiment, except the King's Royal
Rifle Corps, which, however, has four regular battalions.
Between 1780 and 1900 the H.L.I. had fought in forty-eight

main campaigns and battles.

This illustrious regiment came into being in 1777, when Lord McLeod raised it by enrolling 840 Highlanders— 'Gaelic-speaking clansmen of the most primitive and untutored type'. He marched them to Elgin, where they joined 236 Lowlanders recruited in and about Glasgow by Captain Baird. The regiment was soon in India where the flank companies under Captains Lindsay and Baird were sent to the assistance of Colonel Baillie at Conjeveram. Baillie's little force of 3,000 was soon surrounded by the whole of Hyder Ali's army of 85,000 and was under fire from sixty cannons. Reduced to 400, the British force fought it out on a sight rise; even the wounded crawled into position to present their bayonets at the howling enemy horsemen.

The position was hopeless and to save life, Baillie surrendered. But the moment the British laid down their arms they were savagely attacked. The sick, the women and even the children were sword-slashed. Of Baillie's eighty-six officers thirty-seven died and thirty-four were horribly mangled. Of the two companies of Highlanders eighty-eight were killed and 115, of whom only twenty-three were unwounded, were taken prisoner.

They were chained together in filthy dungeons and tortured; Captain Baird was specially singled out for torture. The Highlanders were offered freedom if they would 'curse Christ and embrace Islam'. Not one man weakened and Baird survived to lead the regiment and to be knighted.

At the capture of Cuddalore 'the precious remnant of the 73rd'* as Eyre Coote described them, led the assault. It fought under Cornwallis in the campaigns against Tippoo Sahib, it was at the siege of Pondicherry and in the reduction of Ceylon. The Highlanders were at the capture of the Cape of Good Hope in 1806 and in the Buenos Aires debacle the following year. On the Peninsula, they were with Wellesley (Wellington) at Vimiera and with Moore at Corunna. The regiment joined the Walcheren expedition and in 1810 joined Wellington's army, fighting at Almaraz, Vittoria and various engagements in the Pyrenees. It was also in the Waterloo campaign. Brigaded with English regiments, it won renown at

* So numbered at this time.

Quatre-Bras and Waterloo, where they claimed to have fired the last shot. They captured a battery of guns from the Imperial Guard, then fired one of these guns on the retreating French.

The regiment was in Canada from 1825–32, in the West Indies from 1843–7 and in 1853 it went to Corfu. It did duty at Balaklava and in the trenches before Sebastopol.

The 71st made no recommendations for awards for the Crimean War and succeeding campaigns. H.L.I. officers and those of other regiments strongly opposed the institution of the V.C. and D.C.M. They said that a good soldier needed no inducement to fight harder and no reward if he did so. It was unfair to decorate a man who had been lucky enough to have an opportunity to distinguish himself. Being outstandingly brave was a matter of opportunity, therefore to decorate a soldier would be unfair to others who had not found such an opportunity. There was a lot to be said for this argument.

After a time in Malta, the regiment was ordered to India, by overland route. The journey was arduous, but the hardy Scots enjoyed it. Landing at Alexandria the regiment was forwarded by rail as far as the railway then extended, crossed the desert on donkeys to Suez and arrived at Mhow, via Bombay, more than three months after it had set out.

The regiment had a lot of service in Central India towards the end of the Mutiny, including the capture of Gwalior. It served on the North-West Frontier, Malta and Crete. In 1898, at Candia, it played a conspicious part in quelling the Moslem rising, which ended in the expulsion of the Turks from Crete.

The battalion had an interesting and evocative experience during the operations against the Germans in Belgium in 1945. The men occupied the exact position held by earlier H.L.I. soldiers during the Battle of Waterloo.

The battalion saw three years' service in Palestine after the war, acting as policemen and getting no thanks whatever for their work. The battalion, the last to leave Palestine, lost more than eighty men in guerrilla attacks that were often nothing more than brutal murders; an unarmed British soldier was considered fair game. The battalion won ten decorations during this difficult time.

In 1787 the 74th Highlanders were raised—at the expense of

the East India Company—by Major-General Sir Archibald Campbell, a veteran soldier. The following year they were in India—for eighteen years of tough and varied service. The regiment was several times distinguished during the siege of Seringapatam. It served in the Polygar War of 1800 and in 1803–4 fought at Ahmednugger, Argaum and Assaye, where every officer except one was either killed or wounded. The battalion was reduced to a wreck and for long after was known as the Assaye Regiment. It is one of the two regiments entitled to inscribe both Assaye and Seringapatam among its honours; the other is the 19th Hussars. The battered remnant of the battalion had little rest, but was busy against many freebooters in the Deccan and at the capture of hill-forts.

After Walcheren in 1809, the battalion joined Wellington on the Peninsula. Here it held its position at the front for a long time and in many battles, an outstanding feat as, unlike most other units, it had no battalion at home to feed it with reinforcements. It was present at Busaco, Sabugal, Fuentes d'Onor, Ciudad Rodrigo, Badajoz, Salamanca and Vittoria, various fights in the Pyrenees, the battles of Nivelle, Orthes, Tarbes and Toulouse. Only a Highland regiment, somebody said, could take so much punishment and still keep going at the front.

After peace was made with France, the 74th burnt its old Peninsular colours and the ashes were put in a gold box to be preserved with mess plate.

Between 1818 and 1830 the regiment was in various parts of North America and in Bermuda. In 1834 it was again in Canada, Nova Scotia and the West Indies. They went to the Cape in 1851 for the Kaffir War of 1851–3. The men fought in the wild country of Kaffirland—wading through rushing streams, scrambling up rocky precipices, fighting through the thick gloom of tropical forests. It was a tough war in which a man could not afford to be taken prisoner. Prisoners were cruelly tortured before being killed. The pride of commanding officers in their Scottish regiments was well shown in this war by Colonel Fordyce who, as he died after being shot, said 'Take care of my Highlanders'.

Lieutenant-Colonel Seton of the 74th, was an outstanding credit to his regiment when the troopship *Birkenhead* was wrecked in 1852. Seton was the senior officer aboard the *Birkenhead*, which was taking detachments of ten regiments to Algoa Bay, South Africa, for the Kaffir War. Three Scottish regiments—73rd, 74th and 91st had detachments aboard. In all, the *Birkenhead* carried 631 people—thirteen officers, nine sergeants, 466 men, seven women and thirteen children, apart from the ship's crew.

At two in the morning on 26 February the ship struck. Colonel Seton impressed on the other officers the necessity of preserving silence and discipline; he ordered the troops—nearly all recruits—to parade on both sides of the quarterdeck. A party was told off to work the pumps, another to help lower the boats, another to throw the horses overboard.

Captain Wright, of the 91st, the senior officer to survive, said: 'Everybody did as he was told. All received their orders and carried them out as if embarking instead of going to the bottom. There was only this difference—I never saw any embarkation conducted with so little noise and confusion'.

Colonel Seton stood in the gangway with his sword drawn, seeing the women and children safely down into the cutter, which then put off. Only three boats could be used. When the ship broke in two she began to sink rapidly forward and the men who remained clustered in an orderly way on the poop at the stern.

The ship's commander, Captain Salmond, now shouted that all those who could swim should jump overboard and make for the boats. But Colonel Seton told the men that if they did so they would swamp the boats and drown the women and children. He asked them to keep their places—and they obeyed. The *Birkenhead* was now rapidly sinking. The men shook hands. Moments later they were in the sea.

At no time was there a cry or murmur from the soldiers. Few of them reached the shore; they sank from exhaustion, were killed by sharks or dashed to death on rocks or drowned in the masses of seaweed. In all 438 people were drowned; not a woman or child was lost.

The '*Birkenhead* drill' became famous. The King of Prussia, one of many foreigners impressed by it, ordered an account of the wreck to be read to every regiment of his army.

The immortal example of the *Birkenhead*, inspired by an

officer of the Highland Light Infantry, has since saved thousands of British soldiers and their families in shipwrecks.

The 74th were in India during the Mutiny, then in Malta, Hong Kong and Malacca until 1878. The Army could not afford to leave the regiment out of the Egyptian campaign of 1882 and they fought at Tel-el-Kebir. This campaign was barely over before the 74th was back in India; it took part in the North-West Frontier campaigns of 1897–8 and in the Boer War.

The Highland Light Infantry battalions saw a tremendous amount of tough service in the Great War, well proved by the regiment's sixty-four battle honours and 1,226 decorations.

After its magnificent part in repelling the attack of the Prussian Guard on 11 November 1914, General Willcocks thanked the battalion. He concluded his address with, 'There is no position which the Highland Light Infantry cannot capture'.

At the end of the war the 2nd H.L.I. and a Royal Scots battalion were moved off to the frigid north of Russia and actually took part in some operations around Archangel, a strange theatre of war.

In 1940, with the Camerons, the H.L.I. took part in the tough campaign against a tremendous Italian force of 250,000 in East Africa. The long-drawn Battle of Keren—the capture of what was really a fortified mountain—was the highlight of the campaign and its climax was the capture of Massawa.

The second battalion was prominent in helping to restore order in Greece after the war and stayed there until 1948.

XVII

The Seaforth Highlanders

72ND REGIMENT

1786–1823 The 72nd (Highland) Regiment of Foot. Raised in 1778 as the 78th Highlanders or Seaforth Highlanders; renumbered 72nd in 1786

1823–1881 The 72nd (Duke of Albany's Own Highlanders)

78TH REGIMENT

1758–1763 The 78th Regiment of Foot (2nd Highland Battalion or Fraser's Highlanders). Raised as 63rd in 1757; renumbered 78th in 1758

1778–1786 The 78th Highlanders or Seaforth Highlanders; renumbered 72nd in 1786

1793–1881 The 78th Highland Regiment of Foot (or Ross-shire Buffs)

1881 (July) Seaforth Highlanders (Ross-shire Buffs)

1881 (Nov.) Seaforth Highlanders (Ross-shire Buffs, The Duke of Albany's)

In 1881 the two regiments were amalgamated to become, respectively, the 1st and 2nd Battalions the Seaforth Highlanders. In 1948 the regiment was reduced to one battalion. The Seaforths are now amalgamated with the Queen's Own Cameron Highlanders to form the Queen's Own Highlanders

Nicknames—1st Battalion: the Macraes (at times the Wild Macraes)—2nd Battalion: the King's Men.

IN JULY 1857 the 78th Regiment (2nd Battalion Seaforth

Highlanders) entered Cawnpore. They had marched 126 miles in the broiling Indian heat and had fought and won four separate battles. But they had reached Cawnpore too late; the day before their arrival the survivors of the siege had been murdered.

Of all the massacres in history that of Cawnpore was one of the worst. The Seaforths and the other troops of the small relieving force found that all the women and children, 376 of them, had been foully butchered. The Highlanders were terribly moved at what they saw and they swore vows of vengeance. According to one witness, the Seaforths took strands of hair from the heads of the victims to remind themselves of their vows. Their subsequent behaviour during the Mutiny proved that they exacted vengeance. The Highlanders have always had high respect for women and children and this barbaric violation of them angered them more deeply than description can show.

By the time of the Mutiny the Seaforths were seasoned soldiers. They were a clan regiment of the purest Scottish descent whose two battalions have the same foundation. Both battalions have borne the same number, the 78th, for it was not until after its foundation that the present 1st Battalion became the 72nd, thus leaving the old numeral to the present 2nd Battalion.

The Earl of Seaforth was attainted for taking part in the Rebellion of 1715. Much later his grandson repurchased the family estates from the crown and to show his loyalty offered to raise a regiment (to become the 72nd). His offer was quickly accepted. Many of the men were gathered from the Clan Mackenzie, but the Clan Macrae was so well represented that it came to be popularly known by that name.

So many men possessed identical names that one pay day in July 1778 some men were paid twice and others not at all. It was, in fact, a paymaster's nightmare.

The regiment's first major posting (after service in the Channel Islands) was to India, but it suffered shocking casualties on the way out; Lord Seaforth and 247 men died from scurvy. Of the 975 men who embarked at Portsmouth only 375 arrived fit for duty. It was a black beginning.

The regiment was back to strength by April 1783 when it took part (with the 73rd) in the attack on Cuddalore; then followed Bangalore, Savendroog, Seringapatam and Ceylon. A few days after the taking of Savendroog, the next fort attacked was Outra-Durgum and of this exploit Lieutenant Campbell of the 72nd wrote in his journal:

Lieutenant McInnes, senior officer of the two 72nd companies, applied to Captain Scott for liberty to follow the fugitives up the rock, saying he should be in time to enter the first gateway with them. The captain thought the enterprise impracticable. The soldiers of McInnes's company heard the request made, and not doubting of consent, had rushed towards the first wall, and were followed by McInnes. The gate was shut, but Lieutenant McPherson arrived with the pioneers and ladders, which were instantly applied, and our people were within the wall, as quick as thought, when the gate was unbolted and the two companies entered.

The enemy, astonished at so unexpected an attempt, retreated. McInnes advanced to the second wall, the men forced open the gate with their shoulders, and not a moment was lost in pushing forward for the third wall; but the road leading between two rocks was so narrow that only two men could advance abreast; the pathway was soon choked up, and those who carried the ladders were unable to proceed. At the same time, the enemy threw huge stones upon the Scots who commenced a sharp fire of musketry, and Lieut.-Colonel Stuart, who had observed from a distance this astonishing enterprise, sent orders for the grenadiers not to attempt anything further.

Lieutenant McPherson forced his way through the crowd, causing the ladders to be handed over the soldiers' heads, from one to another, and before the colonel's orders could be delivered, the gallant Highlanders were crowding over the third gateway. The enemy fled on all hands; the foremost of our men pursued them closely, and gained the two last walls without opposition (there were five walls to escalade). The garrison escaped by the south-east side of the fort, over rocks and precipices of immense depth and ruggedness, where many must have lost their lives. By one o'clock, our two companies were in possession of every part of the fort, and McInnes had planted the colours on the highest pinnacle, without the loss of a single man. The Kiledar and two of his people were taken alive. Colonel Stuart declared the business to be brilliant and successful, beyond his most sanguine hopes.

Two companies of the 72nd, Major Petrie's and Captain the Hon. William Maitland's, had captured the fortress and once again Lord Cornwallis thanked the Regiment.

In the early nineteenth century the regiment was in Ireland, the Cape and Mauritius. It returned to India in 1815, but soon after, the regiment was returned to the Cape, where it saw a lot of arduous service during the next four years. It returned to England in 1822 but was back in the Cape by 1828; it had no active service until 1834, against the Kaffirs.

Service in Ireland, Gibraltar, Barbados, St. Lucia, Trinidad and Nova Scotia followed before the Crimea. During 1858 it was at all the engagements of Roberts's division and twenty years later was again with Roberts, this time in Afghanistan for the battles of Peiwar Kital and Kandahar, where the C.O. fell. The battalion fought hard at Tel-el-Kebir.

The 78th, like so many other Scottish regiments, spent its early years in combat in the Low Countries and they suffered in the cold of the winter of 1794–5. At one time they lay for two nights on their arms in the snow. But they forgot about this when they reached the heat of India in 1797.

The 78th had some of its finest service in India—at the storming of Ahmednugger, the great Battle of Assaye (1803) and at Argaum, where it was on the right of the line, and at the storming of Gawilghur.

The internal management of the 78th attracted widespread attention. The battalion was one whose conduct was exemplary and the commandant's method of censure, which replaced crude punishment, was a great success. The commanding officer often threatened to send any bad account of a man to be nailed on the door of his parish church, and he stirred in his men a pride and honour of no ordinary kind. No man wanted it said that he did not do well with Seaforth's 78th regiment, for hundreds of them were from the chieftain's estates, where a love of both regiments of Mackenzie origin was very keen and its honour bright in the keeping of each clansman. There was no such thing as desertion.

During the long-drawn-out wars with France the drain on manpower was immense and many devices were used to obtain men. Regular, militia and volunteer units competed against one another for men—and the Navy was a close rival. Because of this competition the bounties offered for enlistment increased steadily, despite War Office circulars issued to check the practice. A commanding officer who had money used a lot of it in his hunt for men. The 2nd Battalion 78th Highlanders had a recruiting flag* which apparently was used to good purpose. On a large green scroll were the words, in yellow, 'SIXTEEN GUINEAS BOUNTY'. The battalion raised 850 of its

---

* Still in existence in the Scottish Naval and Military Museum, Edinburgh Castle. The battalion was disbanded in 1816.

1,000 men in under eight months, fairly rapid recruiting at that period.

In 1811 the Seaforths took part in Sir Samuel Auchmuty's expedition to Java. In Batavia the grenadier company made itself memorable in the storming of the Dutch entrenched camp at Wettervreden. The storming of Cornelis was another brilliant exploit, but the 78th lost heavily on both occasions.

Six companies of the regiment were aboard the *Frances Charlotte* in 1816 when it was wrecked in the Bay of Bengal, but fine discipline saved most of the men. The regiment was disgusted to lose its baggage and its treasure—worth £2,000.

While this had been going on, a second battalion of the regiment had been in Gibraltar and Sicily and had fought in the remarkable Battle of Maida. They were in Egypt in 1807 and at El Hamet lost their C.O. and 163 men.

During this campaign Sergeant John Macrae, a young man about twenty-two years old, showed that the broadsword in a firm hand is as good a weapon in close fighting as the bayonet. Macrae killed six men, cutting them down with his broadsword. Then he made a dash out of the ranks on a Turk whom he cut down, but as he was returning to the square he was killed by a blow from behind, his head being nearly split in two by the stroke of a sabre. Lieutenant Christopher Macrae, who brought eighteen men of his own name to the regiment as part of his quota of recruits for an ensigncy, was killed in the fight, with six of his followers and namesakes, besides the sergeant. On the passage to Lisbon, in October 1805, Sergeant Macrae had gone to his C.O. one evening crying like a child, complaining that the ship's cook had called him English names which he did not understand, and that he had thrown some fat in his face. Soft and childish in 1805, a warrior in 1807.

Some Seaforths were taken prisoner at El Hamet and many died. But two of the Seaforths, with possibly unsurpassed wit and audacity, not only survived, but rose to high rank in the Egyptian service. Private Thomas Keith became no less a person than General Ibrahim Aga, Governor of Medina, while a drummer became Osman, the so-called 'learned leech' of Alexandria. It seems that he had a rough, a *very* rough, knowledge of first aid, and on this he built a reputation as a medical miracle man. And very well he did financially!

In 1809 the 78th were in Holland to attempt the reduction of Antwerp. At the village of Merxem the Highlanders drove the enemy before them with such conspicuous gallantry that the garrison of Antwerp did not attempt a sortie—the normal thing to have done—and surrendered. Sir Thomas Graham said of the 78th, then composed mainly of recruits: 'No veteran troops ever behaved better than these men, who met the enemy the first time and whose discipline and gallantry reflect great credit on themselves and their officers.' This second battalion was soon to be amalgamated with the 1st Battalion.

The regiment was in Ireland for nine years and later in Kandy, native capital of Ceylon, for nine years. The Seaforths found this duty 'not particularly irksome', as one soldier expressed it. In 1837 when they came home they brought a young elephant, which had been trained to march at the head of the regiment—a living regimental badge. The elephant finished up in the Edinburgh Zoo, where it died. The regiment said its decease was brought about by neglect and they were angry and disappointed.

In the 1840's the regiment was in India. In 1845 they suffered terribly from a cholera epidemic—an ordinary occupational hazard for soldiers in those days. The epidemic killed two officers, 496 men, forty-seven women and 124 children of the regiment. After such appalling casualties the wonder of it is that the regiment could continue to exist. But in 1856 the Seaforths went to the Persian Gulf, where they saw much action before returning to India to help quell the Mutiny.

On 25 September 1857 it was part of the force which advanced to relieve the Residency at Lucknow. The British drove the enemy across numerous gardens until the canal was reached. They crossed by a bridge and the troops entered the streets and fought forward against a fusillade of fire from the houses. The individual work was magnificent. A big force of the enemy attacked the 78th; Captain Hastings of the regiment sprang to the front, there was a Highland rush, and the enemy fled.

Again the enemy came, now with guns, and Captain Webster of the 78th called out: 'Who's for the guns?' Again the Highlanders rushed and the guns were taken. When let loose on the mutineers the 78th did wonders, and Colonel Hamilton often said to Havelock, 'Let them go, sir, and have done with it!'

In the rush the force drew near to the Residency walls, and the advanced guard of the 78th and the Sikhs doubled up, led by Outram, and entered at the Bailey Guard Gate. Later the main body marched in and thus the First Relief was effected.

It was the sound of the pipes—playing 'The Campbells Are Coming'—as the 78th fought its way through the narrow streets, that brought the first news of their relief to the defenders of Lucknow. The conduct of the regiment has been often praised, but praise was seldom higher than that which General Havelock spoke to the 78th Highlanders: 'I am now upwards of sixty years old; I have been forty years in the service; I have been engaged in actions seven and twenty times, but in the whole of my career I have never seen any regiment behave so well as the 78th Highlanders. I am proud of you. I am not a Highlander, but I wish I was one.'

The bravery of the men of Seaforth at this period was the talk of all India, and many awards were made to individuals. So heroic was the work of the regiment that apart from the individual decorations, a Victoria Cross was given to the regiment, but by the unanimous vote of all the men, Assistant-Surgeon V. M. McMaster was chosen to wear it. He had shown great devotion to the wounded on 25 September and spent the whole night under heavy fire, by which act he saved many lives. On the same date Surgeon J. Lee, V.C., did similar work among the wounded Highlanders at the Charbagh Bridge. Another Seaforth man to get the Victoria Cross was Lieutenant Herbert Macpherson, who afterwards became a general and a knight, and was associated with the 72nd Highlanders in the Afghan campaign. He led one of the brilliant charges of the 78th, and was instrumental in capturing two guns.

Havelock wrote: 'In the advance on the Residency the loss fell heaviest on the 78th, which throughout the day was exposed to more fighting than the rest of the force.' It had ten officers killed and wounded out of eighteen and 112 men out of 428.

Sir James Outram 'specially selected' the 78th to cover the retirement of the force. This, today, seems a dubious privilege, but it was an honour in those days. After a break at home the regiment was in Ireland before service in Gibraltar, Canada, Halifax; then back to Ireland, home for a time, and off to India again where it spent many years.

One of the finest fighting soldiers the British Army ever had was a Seaforth—John Mackenzie. He enlisted in 1887 and became a corporal in 1891, but on joining the 2nd Battalion he relinquished his rank. As a private he took part in the relief of Chitral in 1895. He was a corporal again in May 1897, was awarded the D.C.M. and in November that year he was posted to the Lagos Regiment of the West Africa Frontier Force. He was promoted sergeant in 1899. He took part in three campaigns and in each was mentioned in dispatches. He was wounded in the relief of Kumasi and in the Ashantee campaign, during which he won the V.C.

He was attached to a little force of 380 native soldiers, under the command of Lieutenant-Colonel Carter and Major Wilkinson. Moving towards Kekwai on 6 June 1900, they encountered five stockades strongly held by the enemy at Dompoassi.

Officers and men fell fast under the heavy fire and the force was terribly thinned down. Colonel Carter was seriously wounded and Major Wilkinson, wounded but in command, had decided to retire. The gun and Maxims were out of action, ammunition running short, and the enemy's fire as hot as ever. At this point Sergeant Mackenzie came up to him, and volunteered to carry the stockade with the bayonet, if his own company (the Yomba Company, 1st West African Frontier Force) was placed at his disposal. Wilkinson at once ordered up the company, which was in the rear of the column. On the arrival of the first two sections, without hesitation Mackenzie charged at their head, followed by his own men and all others in the vicinity. The enemy fled in confusion and never rallied. Sir James Willcocks, in his dispatch, said: 'It is perhaps not too much to say a disaster to our arms was thus averted, for a retirement under the circumstances might have ended in panic. For this act of distinguished bravery I consider Sergeant Mackenzie is deserving of the highest reward a soldier can receive.'

The following year Mackenzie, now a second-lieutenant, was

again mentioned in dispatches for his work during the Aro expedition; also in 1906 when he was staff-officer of the Munster Field Force and once more during the Kano-Sokoto expedition.

As a major, he was killed in action in June 1915. Fearless under fire, John Mackenzie deserves to be remembered as one of the finest of Scottish soldiers.

During the Great War the Seaforths were early in France and took part in all the main battles, as the list of their battle honours shows. It includes: Marne 1914 and 1918; Ypres 1915, 1917 and 1918; Loos; Somme 1916 and 1918; Arras 1917 and 1918; Vimy 1917; Cambrai 1917 and 1918; Valenciennes; Palestine 1918; Baghdad. Nineteen battalions of Seaforths saw service in the war.

Many rather frightening-looking characters joined the 4th Seaforths and were sent to Bedford for training. Asked where they had come from the men said 'Roos-sha'—Ross-shire. This was said to be responsible for the rumour which flew around that Russian troops were arriving in England.

The 1st Seaforths was the British unit of the Dehra Dun Indian Brigade. At Givenchy in December 1914 the Germans attacked the brigade, forcing back the regiments on the Seaforths' flanks and leaving the Scots in a desperate position. Sir Arthur Conan Doyle wrote: 'The position was dangerous and the Seaforths' losses heavy, but they faced the Germans with splendid firmness and nothing could budge them. Machine-guns are stronger than flesh and blood, but human spirit can be stronger than both. You might kill the Highlanders, but you could not shift them.'

The Seaforths' part in the Loos battle was significant. One battalion of the regiment, the 7th, made a magnificent attack with Camerons, Gordons and Black Watch. 'It was a splendid example of that *furor Scoticus* which has shown again and again that it is no less formidable than the Teutonic wrath,' an eyewitness said. 'Over the parapet, across the open, through the broken wire and over the entrenchment they went like a line of Olympic hurdlers.'

The 1st Seaforths went to Mesopotamia with the Dehra Dun Brigade and fought in several battles against the Turks, before taking part in the victorious entry into Baghdad. But at the

Battle of Sheikh Sa'ad in 1916 they and the 2nd Black Watch had suffered so heavily that the two regiments were temporarily amalgamated as 'The Highland Battalion'. Then, at Sanniyat a few months later this unit lost forty-one officers and 881 men. The Seaforths had good cause to remember the campaigns of the Arabian desert.

The 2nd Seaforths were practically wiped out, too—during the Second Battle of the Somme in March 1918. But a year later the reconstituted unit was in India, where it had a long tour of duty.

Both battalions saw a lot of service in the Second World War. Seaforths, with Black Watch, Gordons, Camerons and Argylls, were prominent at Alamein.

A notable Seaforth man in World War II was Colonel Spencer Chapman, who organized successful resistance activities in Malaya. His regiment saw tough anti-Jap service in Java, where Seaforths had last been in 1811.

At the end of 1944 the Seaforths, as part of the Highland Division, were in Holland when the Germans made their violent counter-attack through the Ardennes. In the process they tried to drown the Highlanders by flooding a low-lying piece of ground at Nijmegen. The Seaforths turned this setback to their own use—as Scots always will. As they waded to higher ground they consoled themselves for their wetting by seizing chickens and geese, marooned by the flood.

A Seaforth motto is *Cuidich'n Righ*, meaning 'Help to the King'. The motto, prominent on the Seaforth badge, was bestowed on the Mackenzies' founder for his bravery in saving King Alexander II of Scotland from the attack of a wounded stag. It is an apt motto, for no regiment has a more loyal record or a more regal past than Seaforth.

XVIII

The Gordon Highlanders

75TH REGIMENT
1787–1809 The 75th (Highland) Regiment of Foot
1809–1862 The 75th Regiment of Foot
1862–1881 The 75th (Stirlingshire) Regiment of Foot

92ND REGIMENT
1794–1798 The 100th Regiment of Foot
1798–1861 The 92nd (Highland) Regiment of Foot
1861–1881 The 92nd (Gordon Highlanders) Regiment of Foot
1881–   The Gordon Highlanders

In 1881 the two regiments were amalgamated, becoming the 1st and 2nd Battalions the Gordon Highlanders. In 1948 the regiment was reduced to one battalion

Nickname: the Gay Gordons

BEFORE THE 75th (Highland) Regiment of Foot came into being, three other regiments had been numbered 75, but it was not until the Highlanders took over the number that it began to mean something. Later, the 75th was to become 1st Battalion the Gordon Highlanders.

When the battalion first went to India, records show that it was subjected to 'a very severe system of discipline' by one of the captains, who was in temporary command, and had received his military education in Prussia. The officer was Robert Crauford, later to be a general; he fell at the head of the famous Light Division at Ciudad Rodrigo. His results with the 75th were hardly satisfactory; Prussian methods applied to Highlanders could not hope to succeed!

The 75th served in the campaigns against Tippoo Sahib in 1791–2, in Malabar and Goa in 1795–7. It was in the Mysore campaign and it fought at Sedaseer and Seringapatam. In 1805 it took part in the assaults on Bhurtpore, then returned home in 1806 after nineteen years Indian service. At this time it received the Royal Tiger badge for its services.

In 1812 the regiment was in Sicily and later it was the garrison of the island of Ponza, in the Bay of Naples—garrison duty of an unusually pleasant type. In 1830 the regiment was in the Cape and served in the Kaffir War of 1835.

In 1849 the 75th went to Bengal—and remained there for thirteen years. During the Mutiny it fought at the siege and capture of Delhi; at Bulundshuhur, Agra and Cawnpore and finally in the advance on Lucknow.

After garrison duty, in the '60's, in Gibraltar, Singapore and Hong Kong the regiment was posted to the Cape; it returned home in 1875. For some time in its career the regiment suffered, as others have done before and since, from uncertainty about its nationality and title. While in India it was assigned the county title of Stirlingshire and was ordered to wear the diced band on the shako and forage cap as worn by Lowland units. Then it was linked with the 39th. In 1881 it again became a Highland unit, the 1st Battalion Gordons.

Amalgamations and changes of title have always plagued and disturbed the British soldier, but somehow, in the end, the troops manage to rise above such irritations. A sense of humour helps. At the time of the great reforms of 1881 the 75th was renamed the 1st Battalion Gordon Highlanders and were equipped with the same uniform as the old 92nd Regiment (2nd Gordon Highlanders); to commemorate the event the officers and men of 'B' Company, the 75th, paid for an obelisk to be erected in the Floriana Gardens, Malta. The epitaph on the memorial runs this way:

> Here lies the poor old 75th,
> But under God's protection,
> They'll rise again, in kilt and hose,

> *A glorious resurrection.*
> *For by the transformation powers*
> *Of Parliamentary laws,*
> *They go to bed the 75th,*
> *And rise the Ninety-Twa's.*

Under this title the regiment had a more interesting time, fighting at Tel-el-Kebir, El Teb and Tamaai. In 1895 it was back in India for the Chitral Relief expedition, a tough but successful frontier war. The experience helped the regiment when it served in the Tirah expedition in 1897–8. It took part in both attacks on Dargai Heights.

Sir William Lockhart said: 'When I gave orders for the taking of Dargai by the Gordon Highlanders, it was said to me that I might as well attempt to take an army up into the clouds. Wherever Scotsmen go, however, we always manage to do very well.'

Field-Marshal Lord Birdwood wrote: 'The action at Dargai made a great impression at the time and not merely on local tribesmen. The newspapers in India and at home were full of the Gordon Highlanders' great charge across the open bullet-swept glacis, and it still delights me to recall the lines of an enthusiastic babu poet who contributed these stanzas to an Indian paper:

> Gallant Gordon Highlanders
> Sent to face the foe,
> Up with their kilts
> When Mathias* said Go!
> The General says the position must be took,
> And all the Gordons with excitement shook. . . .'

Even in England the famous dictum of Colonel Mathias— 'The Gordons will take it!'—became so well known that a wag put up a notice in the hall of a London club: 'Do not leave your umbrella in the hall—the Gordons will take it!'

The 92nd—the 2nd Battalion Gordons—has had a distinguished career and a colourfully Scottish one. The regiment was raised by the Duke of Gordon, but his pretty

---

* The commanding officer.

Duchess had quite a hand in the recruiting. She is said to have placed the bounty between her lips; then she offered both coin and lips to many an eager would-be soldier. 'Now lads, who's for a soldier's life—and a kiss o' the Duchess Jean?' she is said to have cried at the doors of lonely farms and in the market places. I wonder what the women thought about these tactics. Whether the story is true or not, the Duchess certainly worked hard at recruiting; twenty years earlier she had raised a company for her brother to take into the Fraser Highlanders.

The 92nd accompanied General Moore to North Holland, winning its first battle honour in the desperate fight among the sandhills between Egmont and Bergen in September 1799.

It served at Isle Houat (Quiberon Bay) and in the attacks on Ferrol and Cadiz. It was in Egypt in 1801, where it won distinction in the capture of the Tower of Mandora, near Alexandria—an enterprise it shared with the 90th (2nd Battalion Cameronians). It was here that a tailor of the regiment saw a cannon-ball rolling towards him—slowly and ineffectually he thought—so he put out his foot to stop it. The ball carried away his leg above the knee.

The regiment was at Copenhagen in 1807, in the expedition to Sweden and afterwards in Portugal in 1808; with Moore at Corunna in 1809 and later in the Walcheren expedition. In 1810 the 92nd joined Wellington and under the 'Valiant Fassiefern'—Colonel John Cameron—was in enough fights to satisfy even the Highland heart. They included the Battle of Fuentes d'Onor in 1811; the capture of the forts at Almaraz in 1812; the Battle of Vittoria, the fighting in the Pass of Maya in the Pyrenees above Roncesvalles, and the great battles on the Nive in 1813; and the passage of the Gave and the capture of Aire in 1814.

Noticeable at Almaraz among much that was noticeable was the gallantry of Privates Gall and Somerville of the grenadier company who, eager to capture Ragusa, 'tossed aside their bonnets and muskets, dived into the river and swam across' to bring back the pontoon bridge that had been loosened.

The 92nd distinguished itself at Salamanca, too, pushing steadily on through 'the cloud of dust and smoke that rolled along, within which was the battle with all its sights and sounds of terror'.

[147]

At Maya, under Major John Mitchell, they lost two-thirds of their number until the enemy was actually stopped by the heaped mass of dead and dying. Then the left wing of the regiment, coming down from higher ground, was forced to fire at their enemies and their wounded comrades. Napier wrote: 'The stern valour of the 92nd Highlanders would have graced Thermopylae.'

At St. Pierre they attacked furiously, but a storm of artillery beat them back. At this point Colonel Cameron's horse was wounded and fell. A Frenchman ran forward to bayonet Cameron, but Ewen Macmillan rushed up and killed the Frenchman. He carried Cameron to safety, then returned for the saddle. All this was done at the height of the battle, with Macmillan himself under fire. Somebody asked him why he had bothered about the saddle.

'We must leave them the horse's carcass,' Macmillan said, 'but they shan't get the saddle where Fassiefern sat!'

At St. Pierre the 92nd made four distinct bayonet charges. Napier wrote: 'How gloriously did that regiment charge, with the colours flying and its national music playing as if in review! This was to understand war. The man who in that moment, and immediately after a repulse, thought of such military pomp was by nature a soldier.'

Later, with the 50th Regiment, the Gordons routed the French at Orthes and took the town of Aire. For his services here Colonel Cameron received the unusual and marked honour of an heraldic grant; it was, above the cognisance of Lochiel, a representation of the town of Aire. He also received a 'crest of augmentation'—on a wreath a Highlander of the 92nd, up to the middle in water, grasping a broadsword inscribed 92nd and in an escrol above, *Arriverette*, in allusion to Cameron's bravery at the passage of the river.

At Waterloo the 92nd was brigaded with the Royal Scots, the Black Watch and a battalion of the 44th. It was distinguished by its gallantry at Quatre-Bras, where Cameron was mortally wounded. A contemporary writer said: 'Cameron was less the colonel than the chief of that gallant regiment, which was raised partly at Lochaber, his native district. He knew every man in his regiment and watched over their interests as if they had been his brothers or sons. An angry look or stern word from him was dreaded more than the lash. He was their father, and when he fell there rose from his mountain children that wild wail of sorrow which once heard can never be forgotten.'

The Gordons were so infuriated when their chief fell that they charged with furious impetuosity, carrying the French before them. That day they really were irresistible.

At Waterloo a soldier of the 92nd was shot in the thigh by a musket-ball. The ball was extracted, but the wound did not heal and a large abscess formed. A surgeon operated and extracted a five-franc and a one-franc piece, together with a piece of cloth. The larger coin had been hit in the centre and formed into the shape of a cup. The soldier, whose name was Donald, is said to have claimed the coins, straightened out the bent one and spent them both.

The regiment was in Jamaica in 1819 and it stayed there twelve years. It was in Gibraltar and Malta from 1834 until 1841 and in the West Indies for another two years. Between 1851 and 1861 the regiment had a busy life—Corfu in 1851, Gibraltar, Turkey, then India during the Mutiny. They were back in India in 1868, and took part in the Afghanistan campaigns of 1878–80, including the Battle of Charasiah, the operations around Kabul in 1879, the famous march under Roberts to Kandahar and the Battle of Kandahar.

During the Boer War of 1881, the Gordons were in Natal; 120 of them were present at the deplorable action of Majuba Hill. The action reflected no great credit on British arms, but the Gordons held to their positions, repulsing with the bayonet many Boer attacks. *The Times* correspondent wrote: 'The handful of Highlanders was the last to leave the hill and remained there throwing stones down on the Boers and receiving them at the point of the bayonet.' They lost thirty-three killed and sixty-six wounded.

During 1901, Kitchener sent this telegram to King Edward VII:

As Colonel-in-Chief of the Gordon Highlanders your Majesty might be pleased to know that Commandant De Villiers who was present, and has just surrendered, informs me that in the attack on the train on 4th July, at Naboomspruit, the guard of Gordon Highlanders, under Lieutenant Best, who was killed, behaved with the utmost gallantry after the train had been captured by the Boers. The last four men, though surrounded and with no cover, continued to fight until three were killed and the fourth wounded. When the Boers asked the survivor why the British had not surrendered, the soldier replied: 'Why mon, we are the Gordon Highlanders.'*

Other troops might say a thing like this with arrant bravado, but it is easy to imagine the Highlander's air of surprise at such a question. Surrender, like wounds, is not something a Scot much cares for.

More than 9,000 Gordons were killed in the Great War, after which Gordons of one battalion or the other served in Turkey, Malta, Egypt, India, Palestine, Ireland, Gibraltar and Singapore.

During World War II the 1st Battalion fought in France and later in North Africa, Sicily and North-West Europe, helping to spearhead the thrust into Germany.

The 2nd Battalion went down fighting in 1942 when the Japs overwhelmed Singapore, but a new 2nd Battalion took part in the Normandy invasion and the battles which followed. After the two battalions amalgamated in 1947 the Gordons served in Germany, Malaya and Cyprus.

* The Gordons (with the Dublin Fusiliers) took part in more actions of the Boer War than any other regiment.

XIX

The Queen's Own Cameron Highlanders

1793–1804 The 79th (Cameronian Volunteers) Regiment
1804–1873 The 79th (Cameron Highlanders) Regiment of Foot
1873–1881 The 79th (Queen's Own Cameron Highlanders) Regiment
1881–   The Queen's Own Cameron Highlanders
The regiment is now amalgamated with the Seaforth Highlanders to form the Queen's Own Highlanders

CLAN CAMERON was Jacobite and fought for the Stuart cause in 1715 and 1745, but when Britain went to war with France, Alan Cameron of Erracht, Inverness-shire, asked permission to raise a regiment. Later to become a lieutenant-general and a knight, Cameron had an eventful life even for a Scot. Born amid the troubles of the '45, he killed a kinsman in a duel and had to go to America, where he served as a volunteer with the 84th Royal Highland Emigrants during the War of American Independence; when taken prisoner he was treated with great cruelty. Universally popular in the Army, Cameron was known as 'old Cia mar tha', from his practice of acknowledging his men's salutes with the Gaelic greeting *Cia mar tha thu?* (How are you?).

In December 1793 the contingent raised in Lochaber and the surrounding districts assembled at Fort William, where the first parade was held. A few days later Major Cameron marched his men to Stirling, where the regiment received its name—79th Highlanders.*

* It was the third regiment to be numbered 79; the others were not Scottish.

The Letter of Service from the War Office included a clause that men raised for the new regiment would not be drafted into any other regiment—an important proviso with Highland troops. But, as was all too usual, the agreement was not honoured.

The regiment saw active service first in Flanders in June 1794, then went to Martinique for three years, where it suffered from tropical sicknesses and postings to other units; 217 men went to the Black Watch. In 1799 the Camerons were back in Flanders to take part in the bayonet charge on Egmont-op-Zee, with the Gordons.

After duty at Copenhagen and in Egypt the battalion went to the Peninsula, where it lost ninety officers and men in the Corunna retreat; on their return from Corunna the 79th had 700 officers and men down with typhus but they did not lose a single man—surely proof of their toughness—and embarked 1,000 strong for Walcheren six months later. During the whole of the siege of Flushing they were in the trenches without having a man wounded and they lost only one man from fever— the paymaster—when other regiments were decimated by the disease.

Camerons took part in these Peninsular battles: Talavera, Busaco, Foz d'Aronce, Fuentes d'Onor, siege of Burgos, Salamanca, various fights in the Pyrenees, Nivelle, Nive, and Toulouse. At Fuentes d'Onor, Colonel Phillips Cameron, son of the regiment's founder, was killed. He was almost as popular as his father and when he fell the news ran through the 79th and the 71st—*Thuit na Camschronach* (Cameron has fallen)—and saddened the Scots to a degree that can hardly be appreciated today.

At Quatre-Bras the Camerons were selected to cover the British guns, whose men were being picked off by enemy sharpshooters. The regiment charged with the bayonet and drove back the French. At Waterloo the regiment became famous for the gallant way in which it held its square against French cavalry while Piper Kenneth McKay played around the outside. They took part in the final charge which routed Napoleon's crack regiments. But they lost 479 men killed and wounded.

From then until 1836 the Camerons were overseas and

did not see Scotland again; even then they had only a year at home. In the Crimea they were part of the famous Highland Brigade and fought at the Alma, Balaklava and Sebastopol. At the Alma forty-one officers, forty sergeants, eleven drummers and 684 privates went into action. Of these there fell thirty-two officers, nineteen sergeants, four drummers and 424 privates.

At the Alma, Kinglake records: 'Presently, in all the grace and beauty that marks a Highland regiment when it springs up the side of a hill, the 79th came bounding forward. Wrapped in the fire thus poured upon it . . . the hapless Russian column broke and began to fall back in great confusion. The left column was overthrown by the 93rd [Argyll and Sutherland Highlanders] and the two columns which had engaged the Black Watch were in full retreat. . . .' The expression 'bounding on' is a good one, since it aptly illustrates the vigour of any Highland attack.

The regiment endured the agonies of the trenches during 1855. Colonel Clephane, describing the high spirit of the regiment, wrote about a young soldier who, in the agonies of an attack of cholera, refused to retire and held to his post while 'the dews of death were actually on his brow'.

Serving under Sir Colin Campbell, the Camerons were at the siege and final capture of Lucknow, in the Rohilcund campaign and the Battle of Bareilly and other actions. The regiment remained twelve years in India after the Mutiny; during this time four companies fought against the Momunds in the Khyber Pass.

In 1874 a detachment of 130 Camerons served throughout the Ashantee War with the Black Watch. In the '80's the regiment was in Egypt and the Sudan, at Tel-el-Kebir, Atbara, Khartoum and Omdurman.

'It was a noble sight', wrote General Alison, of Tel-el-Kebir, 'to see the Gordon and Cameron Highlanders, now mingled together in the confusion of the fight, their young officers leading with waving swords, their pipes screaming, and that proud smile on the lips and that bright gleam in the eyes of the men which you see only in the hour of successful battle.'

This was where 'Lieut-Colonel Leith danced to the front, waving his sword and crying "Come on, 79th!" and, breaking into double time to the wild music of the undaunted pipers, the regiment, cheering, burst upon the enemy.'

Generally, the relationship among Scottish regiments has always been cordial, but if there is one thing that Jock dislikes it is being tricked out of a fight. At the Atbara in 1898, the battle plan was for the Camerons to destroy the Dervish zariba; then they were to make way for the Seaforths, who would charge through and destroy the Dervishes.

The Camerons knocked down the zariba as planned, but when the Seaforths came up the Camerons were nowhere in sight. They had gone through and done some of the Seaforths' work for them.

Relations between the two regiments were badly strained for more than a year afterwards. The Seaforths might have been a little grateful; the Camerons lost three officers and thirteen men, including Piper Stewart, who had seven bullets in his body. In the advance, Stewart, with the other pipers, had led the regiment to 'The March of the Cameron Men'.

The Cameron men were busy in the Boer War and Colour-Sergeant Farmer won the regiment's first V.C., at Nooitgedacht.

During the Great War the Camerons, despite their limited number of fighting battalions, won fifty-two battle honours.* During the Loos battle the 7th Camerons used the H.Q. flag as a rallying point during the actions around Hill 70. In earlier wars this was standard practice, but it had not happened for many years and probably has not happened since. Nor was it an idle, heroic gesture with the Camerons—the men did rally on the flag and its use was an outstanding success.

In 1923 the 1st Camerons were in Rangoon, where they endured a major earthquake. 'Not that it worried me,' a company sergeant-major said, 'I felt like I was back in France; it was old home week with a Jerry hate.' In 1935 the battalion was in Khartoum.

The 2nd Battalion had a fantastic adventure in 1919, travelling over the wild and dangerous road through the Caucasus to Tiflis on the shores of the Caspian Sea.

---

* Until 1897 the Camerons were the only single-battalion regiment in the Army after the introduction of the new system of 1881. In 1897 a second battalion was formed.

The Camerons were busy with Wavell between September 1940 and February 1941, their finest work being at Sidi Barrani and Nibeiwa. Armour led the way and the Camerons followed in trucks. Showing great initiative, the C.O. gave his orders by loudspeaker and the final one was 'Camerons—Go!' They went all right, with bayonets eager and pipes shrilling. The Italians were killed or they surrendered—mostly the latter.

To the Camerons Egypt was, in a way, a home from home; over 140 years it had become part of regimental tradition. Those who knew the regiment's history were deeply impressed when they passed through Tel-el-Kebir and later when they saw the Atbara River.

The 2nd Camerons, with the 2nd H.L.I. and other units had to fight a force of 250,000 Italians in East Africa and the job took them no longer than nine weeks. But it was hard, gruelling campaigning over broken country, often quite high. In one attack at Keren they had 288 casualties.

When Major-General Klopper of South Africa surrendered Tobruk to Rommel in mid-1942, the survivors of the 2nd Camerons were part of the large force which was captured; The Camerons were possibly the last troops to cease firing.

The regiment was represented by the 5th Battalion at Alamein, fought through Tunisia and Sicily and later was in the fighting in Normandy. Six battalions of Camerons, in all, took part in World War II.

The 1st Battalion represented Scotland in the British Occupation Force in Japan and later went to Malaya. The 2nd Battalion saw duty in Trieste, of all places, before it was disbanded.

The Camerons are possibly the most unassuming of the Scottish regiments. They have always done what was asked of them, without fuss, without complaint.

XX

The Argyll and Sutherland Highlanders

PRINCESS LOUISE'S

91ST REGIMENT

1794–1798 The 98th Argyllshire Highlanders Regiment of Foot

1798–1809 The 91st Argyllshire Highlanders Regiment of Foot

1809–1820 The 91st Regiment of Foot

1820–1863 The 91st (or Argyllshire) Regiment of Foot

1863–1872 The 91st (Argyllshire) Highlanders

1872–1881 The 91st (Princess Louise's Argyllshire) Highlanders

93RD REGIMENT

1800–1861 The 93rd Highlanders; the regiment was formed mainly from the Sutherland Fencibles, enrolled in 1799

1861–1881 The 93rd Sutherland Highlanders

In 1881 the 91st and 93rd were amalgamated, becoming, respectively, the 1st and 2nd Battalions, Princess Louise's (Sutherland and Argyllshire Highlanders). The following year the title was changed to Princess Louise's (Argyll and Sutherland Highlanders). In 1920 the regiment became the Argyll and Sutherland Highlanders (Princess Louise's). In 1948 the regiment was reduced to one battalion

Nicknames: known after Balaklava as the Thin Red Line; also called the Rory's

IN THESE short histories of the regiments I have kept to

chronological order, but in the case of the Argyll and Sutherland Highlanders I have broken away from this rule, for the
regiment has given to the nation a particularly famous tradition
and to its language an equally famous expression—'the thin
red line', though as we shall see, this is really an inaccurate
quotation.

During the Korean War an American correspondent
described the Argylls as 'a fiercely proud and wild lot . . .
speaking a strange jargon completely understandable only to
themselves . . . truly professional killers . . . the cream of
service shock troops. . . .'

No offence to the Argylls but the description, basically, is a
fair one. A century before Korea and a few hours before the
Light Brigade's immortal charge the 93rd (later to become
2nd Battalion A.&S.H.) showed themselves to be fiercely
proud—they proved themselves to be shock troops. The
battalion was the only British infantry on the field at Balaklava
on the memorable 25 October 1854—and they were there
only by chance.

They were in the 1st Division's 2nd Brigade with the
42nd Highlanders and the 79th Highlanders. Following a
ballot, the 93rd was left behind when the rest of their brigade,
with the greater part of the British army, marched away to
assault the fortress of Sebastopol.

The 93rd's job was to protect the town of Balaklava, the
only port controlled by the Anglo-French armies, to help
receive seaborne supplies and to evacuate casualties to the
ships.

The Scots were very upset and angry at missing the opportunity of sharing in the capture of Sebastopol—although this
was to become a drawn-out and terrible siege. Sebastopol was
not captured until long after the action at Balaklava.

The 93rd took up position at the village of Kedikoi, on the
plain north of the port and covering the approaches to it.
They pitched their tents at the foot of a knoll later known as
Highlanders' Hill.

Commander of the Balaklava defences was the Highland
Brigade Commander, Sir Colin Campbell, a veteran of
Wellington's Peninsular War. Campbell sent about two-thirds
of the 93rd to join 800 Royal Marines on a height two miles

right of the 93rd's position. There were British guns on the height, and Turkish guns in trenches and gunpits between the height and the 93rd.

A heavy artillery duel had been fought around the Highlander's camp for about a week and, ready to repel an attack, the 93rd had stood to arms at first light each day.

On 25 October they stood-to as usual. But there was no standing down this time. Unexpectedly, to the right front appeared concentrations of enemy—horse, foot and guns— about 25,000 men altogether.

The 93rd were in line, two-deep, along the crest of the hill with a hundred invalids of the Rifle Brigade and other regiments. On either end of the British line was a battalion of unhappy Turks.

Lieutenant-Colonel Ainslie commanded the British line, but Sir Colin Campbell was there, in front as usual. While he awaited the enemy's movements, Sir Colin could not help seeing how much now depended on the steadfastness of the few hundred men who remained with him.

But he had so much confidence in his Highlanders that he reckoned he could tell them how serious the situation was. He rode down the line, and said: 'Remember there is no retreat from here, men! You must die where you stand!'

The men said: 'Ay, ay, Sir Colin; we'll do that. . . .'

The guns on the height and in the redoubts on the plain kept up continuous fire but the Russian advance continued. Their skirmishers drew close.

The Turkish infantry in No. 1 Redoubt, overrun and driven out, fled towards the British line. Because of this, Major Gordon, commanding the 93rd detachment with the Marines, withdrew his men and marched quickly to rejoin the battalion.

The Russian gunfire was causing casualties to the Scots on the hill-crest and Sir Colin Campbell ordered them to fall back and lie down on the reverse slope.

Four Russian squadrons detached themselves from the mass of Russian cavalry and not expecting a combat with infantry, began their advance. . . .

Suddenly they saw the slender line of Highlanders appear like magic at the top of the hillock.

The impetuous men of the 93rd made a move to rush

forward as though willing to charge and attempt the impossible task of defeating cavalry in an open plain. But Sir Colin shouted fiercely, 'Ninety-third! Ninety-third! damn all that eagerness!' The old soldier's angry voice quickly steadied the line.

The Turks on the flanks of the 93rd's line broke and bolted down the hill through the Highland camp. Here they met a new and terrible foe—a stalwart and angry Scottish wife, with an uplifted stick in her hand. Believing that, besides being guilty of running away, the Turks meant to pillage her camp, she cracked viciously at them. Once she grabbed a strong-looking, burly Turk and held him until she had beaten him half unconscious.

The 93rd watched and laughed until Sir Colin called them to attention.

Famous *Times* war correspondent W. H. (afterwards Sir William) Russell later wrote:

> The Russians drew breath for a moment; then in one grand line charged in towards Balaklava . . . gathering speed with every stride they dash towards that *thin red streak topped with a line of steel*. The Turks fire a volley at 800 yards and run. As the Russians come within 600 yards, down goes the line of steel in front and out rings a volley of Minié musketry.*
>
> The distance is too great; the Russians are not checked, and still sweep onwards through the smoke with the whole force of horses and men, here and there knocked over by the shot of our batteries above. With breathless suspense everyone awaits the burst of the wave upon the line of Gaelic rock; but ere they come within 200 yards another deadly volley flashes from the levelled rifles and carries terror into the Russians.
>
> They wheel about, open files right and left, and fly back faster than they came. Brave Highlanders! 'Well done!' shout the spectators.

The Russians wheeled to their left, as though to turn the British right flank. Campbell ordered the grenadier company of the 93rd, under Captain Ross, to bring the left shoulder forward, and show a front towards the north-east.

Stopped at once by this manoeuvre, and the fire that it brought on their flank, the horsemen wheeled again to the left, and retreated. . . .

---

* The Minié rifle, a French invention, was accepted in 1846 as the regulation weapon for French regiments. In 1851 it was adopted by the British Army. Because of its increased velocity and range, the Minié was a revolutionary development in firearms.

Dr. Munro of the 93rd wrote: 'The men of the 93rd were in excellent spirits, burning to fight; and I do not think there was a single soldier . . . who had an anxious thought . . . or who for a moment felt the least inclination to flinch. The Highlanders were elated and proud to think that under their old Chief and in sight of three armies they had stood to receive a charge of European cavalry.'

Away to the left front of the Highlanders at Balaklava were the Heavy and Light Brigades of the British Cavalry Division. The 93rd had a grandstand view of the incredible and victorious charge of Scarlett's Heavy Brigade, which included their own countrymen, the Scots Greys. They also saw the heroic and hopeless charge of the Light Brigade. The thin red line on the hill-top could be well satisfied with its own part that day.

The two battalions which were to become the Argyll and Sutherland Highlanders had seen a lot of war before the Crimea.

The 91st* were the Argyllshires and they served in South Africa between 1796 and 1802; they were on the Peninsula, fighting at Roliea, Vimiera and Corunna, in the Pyrenees, Nivelle, Bidassoa, Nives, Orthes and Toulouse. They had left Spain briefly to fight in the Walcheren expedition.

The 91st was in Germany and in Holland and was in reserve at Huy while Waterloo was being fought. It served many years in the Mediterranean and later was at St. Helena. Afterwards it spent many years fighting and road-making on the Cape Frontier. The battalion fought in the Kaffir Wars of 1846-7 and 1851-3. Then followed nearly twelve years in India before service in the Zulu War of 1879. Terms in Ceylon and Hong Kong followed before the battalion's part in the greater wars.

It is generally supposed that British operations during the Great War were limited to the Western Front, Palestine and Gallipoli, but, in fact, the 1st Argylls and other Scottish units served in the Balkans.

Between the wars one of the battalion's more interesting duties was to put down a mutiny at Khartoum in 1924.

In the Second World War the Argylls were early in the Desert, under Wavell. They were successful against the

---

* There were a great many Campbells in the 91st. The Army List of 1794 shows eighty-nine officers named Campbell on the active list and seventy-five on half pay.

Italians and their charges were always pushed home hard. But on one occasion they lost nine officers and 144 men when they came up against dug-in artillery at short range. What seemed to worry the battalion most however, was that the pipe-major's pipes were fouled by sand and he couldn't play.

After the evacuation of Greece in 1941 the battalion was sent to Crete to help in an attempt to deny it to the Germans, though weight of enemy numbers and their control of the air defeated the venture.

Later, the battalion had an onerous task during the early landings in Italy. Known as No. 33 Beach Brick, the Argylls, swollen to well over double its usual battalion size, provided protection for the captured beach and organized all traffic through it. When this duty finished they joined the main force and fought right through Italy, taking a major part in the vicious Battle of Cassino.

The spirit of aggressiveness was well shown by Private McKelvie of the 1st Argylls, in Italy. Unarmed, and drawing water from a well, McKelvie was sniped at. He took a dim view of this, so he crawled towards the sound of the firing and by luck found an abandoned German machine-gun, which he fired in the direction of the sniper. Almost at once a wounded German paratrooper appeared with his hands up. Investigating, McKelvie found that he had not only wounded one German, he had killed another. His company commander was a little sceptical until McKelvie produced the body.

The 1st Battalion had three years' police service in Palestine after the war—though conditions were tough enough for active service and both Jews and Arabs took out their spite on the British troops.

The 93rd were the Sutherlands, raised in a remarkable and very unorthodox way. First there was a head-count of all eligible men working on the estates of the Countess of Sutherland. The men received notice that a proportion would be expected to enlist. There was no note of coercion in the notice, which pointed out that enlistment was merely a matter of duty. Parish by parish, Major-General Wemyss paraded the men and moved slowly along the ranks inspecting them. He carried a snuff-box and was followed by a gillie with a flask of whisky. When Wemyss came to a man who impressed him he nodded, the man would step forward and receive a pinch of snuff and rather more than a pinch of whisky, his name was taken and in due time he was called to the colours.

The 93rd was regarded as a family regiment, as many of the men were related and most had been neighbours. They kept this clannish spirit for many years.

Many interesting officers and men have passed through the 93rd's ranks, but one of the most outstanding of its early soldiers was Big Sam McDonald, of Lairg. He was 7 ft. 4 in. in height and broad in proportion. The Countess of Sutherland allowed him 2s. 6d. a day extra pay because she said 'so large a body must need more sustenance than his soldier's pay can afford.'

Sam was so big that he looked incongruous marching in the ranks, so he was told to march at the head of the regiment, with a mountain deer. Once, when serving in Ireland, Sam was challenged to a fight by an Irish giant. Sam accepted, but said that first of all Highland courtesy demanded that he shake hands with his opponent. The handshake ended the fight, for Sam's grip was so fierce that he split the Irishman's fingers and they spurted blood. Sam died while the regiment was on duty in Guernsey.

The 93rd served at the capture of the Cape of Good Hope by Sir David Baird in 1806 and remained there until 1814.

The Sutherland men were 'well grounded in moral duties and religious principles', but there was no religious service in the garrison, except the customary one of reading prayers to the soldiers on parade. The men of the 93rd regiment formed themselves into a congregation, appointed elders, engaged and paid a stipend (collected from the soldiers) to Dr. George Thom, who had gone out with the intention of teaching and preaching to the Kaffirs, and had divine service performed.

While many soldiers were drinking, the Sutherland men danced and their evening meetings were attended by many civilians, unaccustomed at that time to such innocent goings-on in the Army.

The soldiers regularly remitted money to their relations in Sutherland. When punishments were to be inflicted on soldiers the practice was for all troops in camp, garrison, or quarters to be assembled to witness their punishment. But the Sutherland Highlanders were often excused 'as examples of that nature were not necessary for such honourable soldiers'!

When the men disembarked at Plymouth in August 1814, the inhabitants were both 'surprised and gratified'. Regiments returning usually spent all their money in taverns and gin-shops. The Sutherlands were seen in booksellers' shops, buying Bibles, religious books, and tracts and in shops buying gifts to send home. During the short time that the regiment was quartered at Plymouth more than £500 was lodged in one bank to be remitted to Sutherland, apart from many sums sent through the post office.

In 1814—with only a very short rest at home—the 93rd sailed with the expedition against New Orleans, and in the desperate but unsuccessful attack on the Mississippi lost sixty-three killed and 380 wounded.

They were in the West Indies and Guiana from 1823 to 1833, in Canada during the insurrection of 1838 and in North America and the West Indies until 1848.

During the Crimean War they were at the Alma and Sebastopol, apart from Balaklava.* After Crimea, still under Campbell, they served in the Second Relief of Lucknow and in the siege and capture of the city they distinguished themselves repeatedly. In fact the regiment won no fewer than six V.C.s in one day.

Drummer Ross of the 93rd, about twelve years of age but small even for his age, climbed to the top of one of the minarets at the main gate of the Shah Nujjif on the morning of 17 November 1857 and, assisted by Lieutenant W. McBean and Sergeant Hutchinson, he lashed the regimental colour, unfurled, with a feather bonnet on the top of the flagstaff to a spire on top of the dome. This was a signal to the garrison of the Residency of their approaching relief; the Residency defenders acknowledged the signal by lowering their flag. Drummer Ross's action drew a hail of fire from the mutineers.

As if in defiance, Ross sounded the regimental call from the top of the pole. Then he came down, unwounded. This was the only time that the regimental colour was uncased in the presence of the mutineers.

* Three officers and one sergeant were the only members of the regiment to get the clasp for Inkermann when the Crimea Medal was issued: all were on detached duty.

Forbes Mitchell, writing soon after the Mutiny, described the 93rd's advance:

We advanced through the village and came in front of the Secundrabagh, when a murderous fire was opened on us from the windows and flat roof of a two-storied building in the centre of the garden. . . . The Punjabis dashed over the mud wall shouting the war-cry of the Sikhs . . . led by their two European officers, who were both shot down before they had gone a few yards. This staggered the Sikhs and they halted. As soon as Sir Colin saw them waver, he turned to Colonel Ewart, who was in command of the seven companies of the 93rd and said, 'Colonel Ewart, bring on the tartan—let my own lads at them.' Before the command could be repeated or the buglers had time to sound the advance, the whole seven companies, like one man, leaped over the wall with such a yell of pent-up rage as I had never heard before nor since. It was not a cheer, but a concentrated yell of rage and ferocity that made the echoes ring again, and it must have struck terror into the defenders for they actually ceased firing, and we could see them through the breach rushing from the outside wall to take shelter in the two-storied building in the centre of the garden, the gate and doors of which they firmly barred. Here I must not omit to pay a tribute of respect to the memory of Pipe-Major John McLeod, who with seven pipers, the other three being with their companies attacking the barracks, struck up the Highland Charge, called by some 'The Haughs of Cromdale', and by others 'On Wi' the Tartan'—the famous charge of the Great Montrose when he led his Highlanders so often to victory. When all was over and Sir Colin complimented the pipe-major on the way he had played, John said, 'I thought the boys would fecht better wi' the national music to cheer them.'

At this time, said Mitchell, the 93rd was no ordinary regiment. 'They were then the most Scottish of all the Highland regiments; in brief, they were a military Highland parish, minister and elders complete. The elders were selected from among the men of all ranks—two sergeants, two corporals, and two privates, and I believe it was the only regiment in the army which had a regular service of communion-plate; and in time of peace the Holy Communion, according to the Church of Scotland, was administered by the regimental chaplain twice a year.'

One of the most famous and colourful of all Scottish soldiers, whose name, I hope, is still renowned in the Highlands, was a member of the 93rd. He was Willie McBean, an Inverness ploughman before enlistment in the 93rd in 1835, at the age of eighteen. McBean walked with a rolling gait and the drill corporal made some caustic remarks about it. A mate of

McBean's suggested that they get the corporal behind the canteen and give him a good hiding.

A big, strong youth, McBean said: 'Toots, toots, mon, that would never do. I am going to command this regiment before I leave it and it would be an ill beginning to be brought before the colonel for thrashing a drill corporal.'

He rose through the non-commissioned ranks, became an ensign in August 1854 and a lieutenant a few months later in the Crimea. He saw a lot of action during the Mutiny and in the attack on the Begum's palace he took on, single-handed, eleven mutineers—a havildar, a naick and nine sepoys. He killed them all, one by one. By the time he got to the havildar troops were coming to his assistance, but McBean told them to stand off; he fought it out with the havildar and killed him. For this feat he won the V.C. When the decoration was presented to him at a regimental parade, McBean said, 'Toots mon, it didna tak' me twenty minutes'.

McBean kept his word. He rose through every rank from private to command his regiment and retired a major-general —a superb Highlander.

The 93rd remained in India until 1870—twenty-three years was a long time to be away from home, but not uniquely long— and was several times in service on the North-West Frontier. And it was back in India in 1891, for further frontier service.

In 1914, the battalion, now the 2nd A. & S. H., was the first B.E.F. unit to land in France and proud of this distinction they were!*

Between the wars the battalion took part in the actions against the Sinn Fein rebels in Ireland in 1920–2. More colour-fully it provided guards against pirates on the Yangtze River and later was in action on the North-West Frontier in 1935 and 1937.

In the Second World War, the battalion was in Malaya—the only British regiment which had been thoroughly trained in jungle warfare and it had a dangerous and difficult assignment— to cover the withdrawal of frontier posts up to 500 miles from Singapore. It was an impossible mission and the battalion was badly mauled by enemy tanks at Slim River.

* The French certainly appreciated the services of the Argylls in the Great War. They conferred the Croix de Guerre on the 12th Battalion as a whole, a rare honour.

Only a hundred of this ill-fated battalion returned to Singapore and they were the last British troops to cross the causeway which links Johore with the island of Singapore. They came over with their pipes playing 'Hielan' Laddie' and blew up the causeway behind them. Marines from the *Prince of Wales* and *Repulse* were sent to join them; the composite battalion was known officially as the Marine Argyll Battalion, but it has gone down in history as the Plymouth Argylls, the strangest Scottish unit in history. They fought hard and had many adventures but eventually, like everybody else, they were forced to surrender—all but two canny Argylls who evaded the Japs and stayed at liberty—by means known only to themselves—for four years, until Singapore was liberated.

The Argylls' remarkable record in Korea further enhanced their reputation. The highlight of this campaign, from the regiment's point of view, was on 23 September 1950.

In the early hours, two companies were attacking a hill held by the enemy and by eight-thirty had captured one hill and consolidated it. The enemy heavily shelled the hill and under this fire the second-in-command, Major Kenneth Muir, began to evacuate casualties.

By nine-thirty small groups of enemy were infiltrating and this pressure increased, together with increasingly heavy shell-fire and mortar-fire.

The situation became serious, casualties mounted on the captured hill and under the great enemy pressure confusion was possible. At this point Major Muir went to the forward positions and encouraged the men. Their ammunition was running low, too, but an air-strike by the U.S. Air Force was imminent and the men hoped for some lessening of the enemy attack.

The position was clearly marked with air recognition strips and when three U.S. aircraft appeared overhead the Argylls cheered. But their delight was short-lived. The Americans mistook their target and attacked the Scots, first with napalm bombs and then with machine-gun fire. Major Muir made a gallant attempt to prevent a second attack, standing on top of the hill and waving a recognition strip, but his efforts were no use, and soon the top of the hill was a blazing inferno.

The air attack had caused casualties, too.*

The position was desperate. Muir had only three officers and thirty men available to carry on the fight. Forced off the crest by the air attack, he retreated to a position fifty yards below the crest; the enemy had only to move in and take over the hill. Withdrawal was justified and possibly advisable, but Muir noticed that the enemy had not yet moved in and were still plastering the position with heavy fire.

He gathered his men, re-allocated the ammunition—much of which had been lost in the fire caused by the bombs—and said: 'We're going in again.' He gave the remaining officers their orders and then led the indomitable Argylls back up the hill, under a hail of small-arms fire.

For the next half-hour this small party, inspired by Muir, held off a greatly superior enemy force; the men had to pick up loose rounds of ammunition to fire at the enemy. Every minute Muir could hold the hill was valuable in evacuating the new casualties caused by the air strike.

Major Muir's bravery and leadership had already been superb; now it rose to unsurpassable quality. Constantly he moved around his diminishing force, cheering and inspiring them and apparently immune to fire. When he ran out of ammunition for his Sten gun he used a 2-inch mortar against the enemy, until he was hit by two bursts of automatic fire. Mortally wounded, he was carried off the crest and died just below it, his spirit still fighting even though his body was finished. 'The Gooks will never drive the Argylls off this hill,' he said before he died.

He was awarded the V.C. His citation said, in essence, that the effect on the men of Major Muir's splendid leadership was nothing short of amazing and that it was entirely due to his magnificent courage and example and the spirit he imbued in those about him that all the wounded were evacuated from the hill. His actions, the citation added, were 'beyond all possible praise'.

For that matter, so was the conduct of the Argylls generally; they had shown as much courage and steadiness as had their regimental forbears on another hill, nearly a century before.

* It says much for the character of the Argylls that they were not bitter about this tragic incident. It was, they said, one of those risks inseparable from modern war.

XXI

The Test of Battle

THIS BOOK appears to deal more with Scottish victories than defeats. There is a simple reason for this—the Scots, and the Highlanders in particular, have rarely been defeated. Still, they have suffered at the hands of their enemies; some of their units have been annihilated. A regiment faces its sternest test when the going is tough, when everything, including luck, is against it. And everything was against the 51st Highland Divison which fought in France in 1940, before the French collapse. During the Great War an earlier 51st Highland Divison had made a spectacular name for itself, which became legendary in Scotland, and the division of 1940 had a lot to live up to—the reputation of its predecessor as well as hundreds of years of history.

In Edinburgh on 20 June 1940 General de Gaulle said: 'I can tell you that the comradeship in arms experienced on the battlefield of Abbeville in May and June 1940, between the French Armoured Division, which I had the honour to command, and the valiant 51st Highland Division under General Fortune, played its part in the decision which I took to continue fighting on the side of the Allies unto the end, no matter what may be the course of events.'

So much happened later in the war that the deeds of the 51st in 1940 never received much publicity. Perhaps, too, this was partly because the 51st fought independently of the British Army during those difficult days. In May it was fighting near the Saar; a month later it was within sight of the sea and the remnants of two of its brigades surrendered in the little town of St. Valéry-en-Caux. It was beaten, but how it struggled to live!

Three brigades—nine battalions—made up the infantry section of the 51st; two battalions each of Seaforths, Gordons, Argylls and the Black Watch, and one battalion of Camerons.

Lodged in French towns and villages near the Belgian border, the Scots made friends with their hosts; their pipes and drums played for local gatherings; they collected money for children of one village; they gave parties. They were as well regarded as the Highlanders of Waterloo days.

In April 1940 the division took over a sector on the Saar front, the only British division to do duty there. And it was pleasant duty, at first, for the weather was fine and the countryside magnificent—in places, just like Scotland. By 1 May the Black Watch had been in action, beating back a fierce attack on some forward posts. The battalions took their turn in the line and the skirmishing became more bloody— miniature battles. Division H.Q. said that routine patrolling should be carried out in such an enterprising way that deliberate raiding should be unnecessary. The patrols were enterprising all right. Led by enthusiastic young officers, they hit out and hit hard—rather irritating the French troops, most of whom were all for a policy of live and let live.

On 10 May the Germans opened their attack on the Low Countries and action along the 51st's front quickened. On 12 May a Black Watch platoon holding the village of Betting was heavily attacked. The village was in flames the following night when a fighting patrol of Gordons rescued the Black Watch. By the end of next day many of the Gordons and the Black Watch had been blooded; some of them fought against storm-troopers and found the much vaunted supermen pretty tame.

The Seaforths and Camerons had also been in action. At this time the Germans made a practice of tapping the forward Scottish telephone cables, but that didn't help them much; the Camerons spoke in Gaelic.

On 14 May over a ninety-minute period the Germans fired 3,600 shells into a one-company front of the Gordons, but the Gordons fought off the enemy infantry attack which followed. And by now the Argylls were in action as well. The battle was now intense and furious and the Scots had to withdraw to maintain a front with the French forces on either flank.

The Highlanders were showing a lot of dash and fighting spirit and General Conde, commanding the French Third Army, referring to the Highlanders' 'hard fighting qualities and high morale', said that the Highlanders of 1940 had renewed the tradition of Beaumont-Hamel.*

Originally the division was to be used for the defence of Paris—a high compliment—but plans were subject to rapid change. On 29 May the division was in position on a twenty-mile front in the region of the Somme, Bresle and Bethune rivers. While the 51st, with French troops, was mounting an attack the last remaining fragments of the B.E.F. were being ferried home from the beaches of Dunkirk—an enterprise which also has obscured the fighting retreat of the Highlanders.

Early on the morning of 4 June the Scots moved out to the attack—and, by an unlucky coincidence, the Germans had prepared an attack for the same time. A company of Camerons met a German battalion in a rye-field and took them on. Forty men survived the fight and the one officer remaining, a second-lieutenant, leading his men to a wood, asked for more ammunition so that he could push on to the objective. The lieutenant needed a lot of convincing that his task was hopeless. Fifty men of another company survived and fought it out with German infantry.

On 4 June a battalion of Seaforths, among other Highlanders, were attacking German positions at Mont de Caubert. When the supporting French tanks were knocked out the Seaforths went on without them—into withering machine-gun fire which mowed them down like grass. In one platoon Sergeant Donald McLeod was the only man to reach the objective—and he was badly wounded. Left alone on the ridge he eluded the enemy for two days and nights and finally rejoined his battalion. David Ross, reported missing, turned up two days later with sixty Cameron Highlanders whom he had led through twelve miles of enemy-infested country. Lieutenant Hugh Macrae lay on the field until dark, then collected all the wounded who could walk or hobble and led them out of trouble.

---

* Where the earlier 51st Division had made itself illustrious. On high ground near Beaumont-Hamel is a granite cross to the 8th Argyll and Sutherland Highlanders.

The Seaforths and Camerons lost twenty officers and 543 other ranks in the day's fighting. They had been faced by close machine-gun fire, mortars, artillery and dive-bombing. The official report said: 'The Highlanders did not spare themselves; they had been signally unwilling to admit defeat and when defeat could no longer be denied, they often maintained a stubbornly independent attitude to it.'

Two battalions of Argylls were heavily attacked; one company was surrounded by 1,000 enemy infantry. A second-lieutenant named Green, with the battalion for only one day, was ordered to hold with his platoon the crossroads at Arrest. Green was not heard of again, but he held the crossroads and put a high cost on them before he was overrun.

The front was so long and its defenders so few that it was a physical impossibility to hold it against the overwhelming numbers of Germans, but at no point was the front abandoned without fighting.

At one point the Black Watch was holding a front of two and a half miles; they were well placed with good fields of fire and they caused the Germans heavy losses. The Lothian and Border Horse, too, had been in action and some of the Argylls had been scrapping fiercely in village streets.

On the afternoon of 5 June 200 Camerons were crossing clover fields when they were attacked by successions of dive-bombers. The only protection was to lie down, which the Camerons did. Then they fell asleep—and not one of them was wounded.

On 6 June the village of Frenleu became the scene of a stubborn, heroic fight by the Argylls. Despite the heavy German attack, including heavy mortars, the Scots held the village and twice they drove back an extended enemy rush. But casualties mounted steadily and before long the cellar of the village school was full of wounded men.

The Argylls' only mortar was hit and in the heat of the summer's afternoon German reinforcements arrived—three tanks, motor-cycle troops and 400 infantry. At five o'clock a mortar shell blew up the last ammunition truck and wrecked the battalion headquarters. An hour later, the position hopeless, the survivors made a run for it in some trucks and two carriers. Two soldiers and the regimental padre had volunteered to stay with the men too badly wounded to be moved.

The padre had cared for the wounded all that day, even going out under fire to get water for his patients. When night fell the Argylls had lost twenty-three officers—including the C.O. who stood his ground—and more than 500 men. Seven officers and 182 men forced their way through the enemy.

It was obvious now that a fighting rearguard action was all that could be hoped for. The Scots had neither the men nor the ammunition and as somebody said, 'the Germans could no more be contained than water in a basket'. And water, for many of the Scots, was as short as sleep.

One brigade, the 154th—Black Watch and Argylls—fought all day on an eight-mile front and at the end was down to fifty per cent of its strength. The 152nd Brigade was mutilated.

Two companies of Argylls, previously cut off, rejoined their brigade on 8 June, after fighting, scheming and bluffing their way through German territory. On that day it was realized that a steady rearguard action would not be enough; to avoid encirclement the division must withdraw swiftly and firmly. The battalions were taken back during the night of 8-9 June. The plan was for 23,000 men of the division to embark at Le Havre, but the situation was desperate and evacuation could not begin until 13 June, because those French who were still fighting could not move quickly, having no motor transport. General Fortune, commanding the 51st, could have got his own men quickly to Le Havre, but to retire at speed would expose the flank of the French 31st Division. The general, loyal to his obligations, waited.

The situation developed alarmingly. On 10 June, the date of Italy's entry into the war, the exhausted men of the Black Watch occupied a position on the Varenne River. For ten days they had been constantly in action. 'But somewhere within their dreadful weariness lay a reserve of strength, a fount of valour that was to carry them through another day, and yet another.'

That day they were in close action again, as the Germans advanced behind a screen of refugees. The Black Watch had orders to hold the river until nine o'clock. They held it. Then came orders to hold it until ten; they did so. Then eleven. Finally they pulled out—but before they moved they destroyed most of their equipment, including their tartan trews. 'No bloody German's going to put his fat arse in my trews!' a corporal said savagely as he ripped them with a bayonet.

On the morning of 10 June the idea of evacuating from Le Havre had been abandoned; the alternative was St. Valéry-en-Caux, a poor port. The division formed a box-like perimeter around the little port; there to await the Navy, which had promised to do its best.

The French were supposed to form part of the box, but many French troops were now undisciplined and in open flight. Still, by nine o'clock on 11 June the box was formed and the Highlanders, still cheerful, prepared for another last stand. Time was now running out and the Germans were moving fast. At this time the Lothian and Border Horse managed to help stabilize the situation at desperate points, though they lost some tanks doing it.*

On the east the Seaforths and Gordons had been heavily engaged and had suffered casualties. Black Watch men on a forward slope with little cover and their right flank bare had no rations until they found some biscuits and killed a cow. The Black Watch fought hard that afternoon against steady and stiffening German pressure and by six o'clock fifty men were dead or wounded. They were assisted at one point by a squadron of tough French cavalry.

The Germans attacked the box and penetrated it on the western side. The Seaforths, outranged by enemy weapons, stood up to a lot of punishment. German tanks went through them in the wood at Le Tot, though the Germans paid for the passage. They took a commanding hill from the French and soon there was fighting about the south-western outskirts of the town. That evening the Germans were hovering around the town, ready to pounce.

Embarkation was to begin at ten-thirty that night, 11 June, and orders were sent around that troops would assemble in the town; the Seaforths did not receive the order and stayed in the wood. At night the town was almost a shambles and most of it was on fire, and packed with troops. But no ships arrived. The

---

* A battalion of Royal Scots Fusiliers, though officially pioneers, fought well as infantry during the campaign.

ships had been waiting off the coast since the afternoon of 10 June, had entered St. Valéry that night and had left in the morning. The ships had then assembled north of the harbour before midday on 11 June; here they were attacked. That night, despite heavy machine-gun fire from the cliffs, the ships took off from beaches east of St. Valéry about 1,400 British and 950 French soldiers.

On 11 June evacuation of Le Havre* commenced and orders to evacuate at St. Valéry came from the Admiralty at the same time. But it was now too late. Still, some soldiers were taken off, with loss to the Navy; a sloop was sunk close to St. Valéry. There would be no evacuation that night. The troops, in the darkness and rain, took this blow calmly and uncomplainingly and moved out to defend the perimeter for another day. Discipline, both imposed and personal, was as high as ever, though hope was now failing.

At 3.30 a.m. on 12 June the Germans sent an envoy into the Seaforths at Le Tot wood. The 51st Division had surrendered, the envoy said and suggested that the Seaforths do likewise. The Seaforths asked for time to consider. Many of their men were badly wounded and needed medical help; these men, with volunteers to support or carry them emerged from the woods and made for the German lines. The remainder of the battalion lay hidden in the wood all day and that night, in small parties, they tried to break through—but very few finally escaped.

Nearer to St. Valéry a second-lieutenant of the Gordons took command of the situation at a small village and with great energy and initiative organized the defence. A renegade French officer came in with a message for him demanding surrender. The young lieutenant gave him a loud and very rude reply. 'Take that to your German general,' he said. He held out for a long time until overrun.

The situation in the district was chaotic, with refugees and their pitiful transport crowding the roads, with Germans attacking everywhere and with everything. About eight o'clock on the morning of 12 June about 140 men of the Black

---

* The 154th Brigade of the 51st Division was evacuated from here. After the surrender some Highlanders managed to evade their guards and eventually returned to England by devious routes.

Watch reached St. Valéry to take up their position to the north-east; here and on the east General Fortune had decided to make a last stand. At 8 a.m. that morning, also, the French officially capitulated.

Camerons, Gordons, Seaforths and Black Watch organized their final resistance. Dead tired, but disciplined, with typical Scottish resolution they went about their task. There was now no hope; the Germans dominated St. Valéry and the Navy could not enter. Only a fragment of the division remained —the once stout trunk of it had been whittled down to a narrow stick. There was not a round of ammunition for the guns; the Sappers had no stores; food was scarce. General Fortune made a brave decision; he surrendered.

When the Black Watch men heard the news, they wept. They couldn't believe it. But the decision kept many of them alive, for they could only have perished had they fought it out. One detachment, in fact, went on fighting until individually commanded to surrender. Not long after this what was left of the Gordons, unarmed, marched past General Fortune and gave him 'Eyes Right'.

The significant fact about the end of the division is that it remained a division until the death; a unified force, disciplined and aggressive. All around them was defeat, rout, uncertainty and cowardice. But the Highlanders stood firm and even when defeat was evident to their reason their spirit rejected the idea. The B.E.F. was smashed and the epic of Dunkirk was over, yet the Highlanders' initiative and their sense of responsibility as soldiers remained unimpaired—more than that, these qualities were heightened. There had been many individual platoon and company adventures of great daring.

It seems pointless to say that the 51st was a good division; all Scots divisions are good. But the 51st *was* very good; it stood up to disaster as well as to triumph. These Scots had proved themselves to be soldiers worthy of their splendid ancestors.

In the Castle at Edinburgh is one of the most magnificent war memorials in the world, keeping alive the service and sacrifice of Scottish soldiers. Before conscription became law in 1916, more than 500,000 Scots had volunteered. Just 100,000 were killed in the Great War and their names are recorded today in the Edinburgh memorial. For many, many more thousands who have died abroad over the centuries there is, and can be, no memorial. But in the Presbyterian Church, Singapore, on a memorial tablet to the Argyll and Sutherland Highlanders, is an inscription that might well apply to all Scottish soldiers who fought and fell.

The memorial reads:

To the everlasting fame of the Officers and Men of the 2nd Bn. The Argyll & Sutherland Highlanders 'The Thin Red Line' who served during the Malayan Campaign 1941–42

244 fell in action
184 died as prisoners of war
Their bearing added lustre to the name
Of their regiment, and of their country

Still, when a chief dies bravely
We bind with green one wrist,
Green for the brave. For heroes
one crimson thread we twist.
Say ye, oh gallant hillmen,
for these, whose life has fled,
Which is the fitting colour,
The Green one or the Red?

ACKNOWLEDGEMENTS

Apart from the many books specifically mentioned in my book as sources of reference I have referred to many other volumes. My book would not have been possible without the labours of these earlier historians. These are the main books consulted:

Bell, D., *Soldiers of the King* (Hammond, Hammond), 1948.

Chichester, H. M., and Burges-Short, G., *Records and Badges of the British Army* (Gale & Polden), 1900.

Forbes-Leith, W., *The Scots Guards in France* (William Paterson), 1882.

Grant, J., *British Battles on Land and Sea* (Cassell), 1899.

Lawrence Archer, Major J. H., *The British Army* (George Bell), 1888.

Linklater, E., *The Highland Division* (Ministry of Information), 1942.

Low, C., *Battles of the British Army* (George Routledge), 1890.

Maxwell, Sir Robert (editor), *The Lowland Scots Regiments* (James Maclehose), 1918.

Richards, W., *Her Majesty's Army* (J. S. Virtue), 1900.

Settle, J. H., *Anecdotes of Soldiers* (Methuen), 1905.

Tucker, A. B., *The Romance of the King's Army* (Henry Frowde and Hodder & Stoughton), 1908.

Scotland For Ever, The Gift Book of the Scottish Regiments (circa 1915).

The Scottish Regiments (Oliver & Boyd), 1942.

I have referred also to a large number of regimental histories of various dates.

I wish to thank my friend, Captain R. G. Hollies-Smith, F.R.G.S., of the Parker Gallery, Albemarle Street, London, W.1, for his courtesy in making available to me many of the illustrations used in this book, including that for the jacket. I should also like to thank the Royal Highland Fusiliers, King's Own Scottish Borderers, Black Watch, Scots Guards, Gordon Highlanders, Argyll and Sutherland Highlanders, Cameronians and the Royal Scots Greys for their help in the preparation of this book, in particular for providing material for some of the illustrations.

Index